SOLO

Explorers

Inspiring Stories of Women's Courage and Transformation Through Solo Travel

VAISHALI PATEL

BALBOA.PRESS

A DIVISION OF HAY HOUSE

Balboa Press books may be ordered through booksellers or by contacting:

Balboa Press
A Division of Hay House
1663 Liberty Drive
Bloomington, IN 47403
www.balboapress.co.uk
UK TFN: 0800 0148647 (Toll Free inside the UK)
UK Local: (02) 0369 56325 (+44 20 3695 6325 from outside the UK)

Print information available on the last page.

ISBN: 978-1-9822-8753-5 (sc)
ISBN: 978-1-9822-8754-2 (e)

Balboa Press rev. date: 11/10/2023

"Not all who wander are aimless.
Especially not those who seek truth beyond tradition,
beyond definition, beyond the image."
Betty Warren, Mona Lisa Smile

CONTENTS

Passion and purpose-led solo travel transformation:

Work-based solo travel transformation:

Key relationships that caused a transformation:

DEDICATION

I dedicate this book to my mother.

INTRODUCTION

By stepping out of your comfort zone, facing your fears, meeting fascinating people, and overcoming problems on your own, solo travel is one of the best ways to learn about yourself and the world at large. Travel gives us the greatest gift of all: the ability to change our lives. Travel can be compared to an elixir for the soul. A single trip has the potential to transform your life by providing you with the opportunity to embark on an inner journey of personal growth through self-reflection.

Travelling allows us to disconnect from daily routines that often keep us trapped in what we know. It allows us to reset and reflect on how we see ourselves by putting ourselves in unfamiliar situations and environments.

When we travel, we gain the ability to appreciate humanity in people. We learn to identify and respect the similarities we share with people from diverse cultures.

Unfortunately, women are sometimes discouraged from travelling alone, particularly to certain parts of the world.

As an Indian woman growing up within a conservative family, solo travel was not encouraged due to cultural expectations. I chose to break the mould in 2010 and embarked on a solo travel adventure for nearly two years. I faced fears of how I would handle unforeseen situations, striking up conversations and making friends, and finding my way around a country on my own. I have since travelled solo extensively over the last 10 years for work and play. I believe, as we step outside our comfort zone through solo travel and learn more about ourselves and the world, we develop life skills and capabilities such as self-trust, self-reliance, and resilience, all of which help us become better people and leaders in life.

These leadership and life skills often get overlooked in our society. Travel is often seen as a fun, sociable, or relaxing activity and not truly recognised for its contribution to a person's development. Can you remember the last time an interviewer asked you what life skills you took away from a lengthy trip? One intention for creating this book is to show how travel can be incredibly empowering at a personal and professional level.

Another reason for creating this book is because I wanted something that women who want to travel solo can gain inspiration, courage, and empowerment from, through the storytelling of other every day, brave women that have taken that journey. I wanted to give a voice to incredible female role models with remarkable stories. I chose to feature women from different life stages and backgrounds, so that readers can find a story that they can see themselves in.

Some intrepid solo female travellers who've seen and done it all are here to disprove the stereotype of the frail lone lady abroad. They're eager to share their stories of difficulty and victory to inspire other women to go on their transforming solo travels.

I felt energized when interviewing the women for my book. As I listened to them relive their experiences, it was wonderful to see them reconnect to the triumphs, joys, and moments of reflection and deep connection they experienced. This was the most special part of creating the book.

The allure of travel is such that no matter how many stories you read, how many photographs you see, or how much homework you do, you never know what you'll get or how it will affect you. Every place, person, and experience is unique, and travel provides endless opportunities for personal development. Your life experiences will have a lasting impact on how you see the world and how you choose to live in it, whether you recognize it or not at the time.

If you are considering travelling on your own and are looking for inspiration or have fears, then this book is for you. You can follow from beginning to end if you are a structured reader. Alternatively, you can open the pages to the life lesson or person who most speaks to you. Think of it like a menu of lessons and stories.

You will learn that you're not the only one that has fears and concerns about safety, your ability to handle situations, and being alone. You will discover the many women of different ages, backgrounds, and careers, who have travelled solo despite these concerns and went on an inner journey that transformed their lives.

I share the transformational stories of thirty women that have travelled solo and the profound impact it had on their life choices. I reveal the experiences, wisdom, and tips that can empower women who are afraid of the unknown to leap, making this both a deeply moving and practical book.

One thing I would like to stress to you, my dear reader, is about expectations and comparisons. Like that yoga teacher always says at the beginning of any class, "Don't compare yourself to others," the same is true here. For some of us, a breakthrough may be creating an NGO on our travels, for others, it may be being able to follow a map (don't ask me about my map-reading skills!). This is your journey of exploration. By the time you finish reading the book, you'll be ready to book your ticket, have a loose plan in place, make connections before you've even landed, feel confident, and trust yourself that you can do it. You will be ready for the adventure. We hope these tales have piqued your interest in continuing your journey and learning what enchantment awaits you next.

For those of you who have already embarked upon meaningful solo adventures, I hope this book provides you with a chance to reflect. Sometimes, we miss the lessons, and by reading these stories, I hope it helps you to recall and embody those big or small victories.

I'm truly thankful to Women in Travel CIC for making my book possible through their generous sponsorship.

Women in Travel CIC is a UK-based, award-winning social enterprise that connects diverse, underserved female and non-binary talent to employment and enterprising opportunities in the travel, tourism, and hospitality industry.

http://www.womenintravelcic.com

Explore a variety of free resources at www.solo-explorers.com to enhance your solo travel experience.

CALL ME CRAZY

Vaishali Patel

People called me crazy when I booked my tickets to Rio de Janeiro; I was flying in three weeks. I could hardly believe it myself because Brazil was not a country I had a strong desire to go to for anything but the Rio Carnival and Amazon rainforest. However, the calling to go there was so strong that I chose to put my rational mind aside and trust that inner calling. Sometimes, when we act based on our gut, our actions don't always make sense.

I had never travelled the way I chose to travel around Brazil before. I chose not to plan this trip with daily schedules and joining group tours despite being told about how unsafe Brazil was. I had a deep innate knowing that somehow, I would be ok if I took care of the basics. I chose where to go based on my interests in music, dance, culture, and nature. I felt so alive, excited, and grounded when researching things to see and do online. I booked key flights between cities such as Rio de Janeiro to Bahia on the east coast, then to Natal in the northeast, from Jericoacoara in the north to Manau on the west coast, and then from there back to Rio on the east coast. I chose to figure out what I did in those destinations when I got there.

I wanted to feel authentic Brazil and one way I knew to do that was to live with the local people where possible. I love experiencing the culture of a country through its people, their customs, and their daily lifestyles, including where they shop, eat, and relax. I had used the CouchSurfing site in New Zealand and enjoyed my experience of getting to know people by living with them, sharing stories, and repaying them with a cooked meal. I chose to do the same in Brazil, despite my fear of the unknown. I looked

1

for people that had lots of positive reviews and read lots of them before booking an apartment on Copacabana beach for the first three nights.

It was 6.45am when the taxi pulled up outside the CouchSurfing apartment I was staying in. I could not believe my luck when I got out and looked at the beautiful array of red, orange, and purple colours in the sky over Copacabana. My CouchSurfing apartment was right on the beach with windows going along the whole length of the living room; it was paradise.

After putting my luggage in one of the bedrooms, I chose to go out for a little walk along Copacabana beach. I told the lady that maintained the home that I'd be back in an hour. I walked along the beach, taking in the sights of the mountains, the smell of the sea, and people working out on the beach. I came across a map and saw that the Sugarloaf mountains were within walking distance and decided to walk there, taking in the views of Rio. When I got there, I took the cart up to the top and took in the panoramic views of the city with a mango ice cream in one hand.

I walked back to the apartment at 7pm and the housekeeper was shocked that I had walked the streets of Rio by myself. She thought I was crazy as it was unsafe to walk the streets alone. It was an epic start to my trip and set the foundations for how I would travel for the rest of my time there. I'd wake up in the morning and ask myself, "What would you like to do today, Vaishali? Where do you want to go?"

The next morning, I decided I want to see the favelas of Rio. Favelas are 'slums' or 'shanty towns' that were built by soldiers from Bahia as there was a lack of affordable housing for them in Rio. I found a guy offering tours of the Rocinha Favela, the largest in Brazil, on the CouchSurfing website. He was teaching English in a school for young children in the favela and decided that it would be a more authentic experience with him than going via a tour company. Along with five other people, I sat on the back of a motorbike and rode up to the top of the favela to a shop where we stood at a lookout point. I was shocked to see houses built on top of each other and dainty ladders made to climb to another floor of the house on top of a tree. There were big blue tanks on top of roofs to gather water. I saw boys sitting on corner bends, looking like they were just chilling, but they were scouting for the police.

I turned to our guide and asked when we would go to see the slums. He told me that this was it. I was a bit surprised as I saw clean streets and nice artwork painted on the walls. It just didn't meet the expectations I had in my head of what a slum would look like. He then asked me if I would like to see the unofficial tour where we can't take photos or the official one to continue. I said the unofficial one and the others agreed. That was a real eye-opening experience. The back streets were narrow and uneven and there were potholes everywhere. I saw bullet holes in the walls with piles of trash scattered about.

Seeing the real favela made me appreciate the safety and ease of living in London and my home. Seeing the bullet holes in the walls and the unpredictability of when a gun shooting might happen frightened me. The gangs that run the favela protect the people that live there. No one's allowed to rape anyone. No one's allowed to steal anything from anyone. But if you stepped outside the favela, they couldn't guarantee that level of protection. Within the favela where there are unpredictable shootings, people are safer than outside the favela. I was surprised by that.

People didn't have lavish or stable homes, but they looked content and happy, knowing they were supported. I saw people come together to carry a sofa up a steep road to take it to a house. I saw elderly people walk up and down steep roads, and I would wonder how safe they were when it rained. I appreciated how resourceful they were, despite not having many resources.

I discovered my internal resource of courage, too, not only in where I went but also in the physical activities I took on. It was one of the biggest transformations of that trip. I arrived in Natal, in the Northeast of Brazil, and was staying with a lady that I found on Airbnb. She was Brazilian but had lived in London for many years and decided she would come here and build a home that overlooked the sea, which she did. One morning, she told me she was going surfing and asked me if I wanted to come. I felt this dread in my stomach as I'd never surfed before, didn't think I could balance on a surfboard, and wasn't a strong swimmer nor could I tread water. She told me the beach had surfing lessons; so, in the spirit of adventure, I decided to give it a try.

I was scared but I had a supportive and encouraging teacher and was able to stand on the board and get my balance. Slowly, I was able to slightly surf a slow wave and I felt this excitement in me as I started to believe that I could do it. I must have fallen off the board 10 times that day and surfed three waves. The pivotal moment was when the teacher told me to stand on the board and then suddenly, he pushed me off. I was not expecting that. He said, "That was your biggest fear, wasn't it? That you'd fall into the water? And you're still alive." When I got onto the surfboard after that, I didn't feel that fear. The next day, I surfed 10 waves and fell off just three times. I was like a little girl full of elation and joy. It was just the most incredible feeling to do something I thought I couldn't do and enjoy it.

Whenever I look back at those surfing pictures, I remember the thought I had before, that I can never do that, and I did do it. Sometimes, it's about having the right teacher who believes in you and helps you face your fears. I always smile when I think about that experience and remember that adventurous streak in me.

I bring this sense of adventure into my day-to-day life by doing the things that scare me. I also won't stop if I've "fallen off the board" as much as I used to and my relationship with failure has changed. When I returned to London, I decided to go for it and started creating self-development workshops that use movement and creativity to help people discover and unleash their authentic selves.

Before Brazil, I was a stickler for planning and visiting must-see sites. I did little of that in Brazil — I was there to experience the land. It was a very spiritual journey for me. I couldn't explain to anyone what it was. I discovered that Brazil's essence was very feminine, and I was drawn to the water, which is linked to our emotions. I felt completely safe in this country where it's supposedly not safe. I didn't know anyone, but I made connections everywhere.

I had an interesting experience in Pelourinho, Salvador. After a walking tour of the beautiful, cobbled streets, my guide turned to me and asked me if I'd like to witness a local spiritual ceremony called Candomblé. I had never heard of this and was intrigued as it sounded cultural and authentic. I took a taxi with him and three other people. We walked upstairs to a house, and I saw people dressed in white. A man was sitting at one end of the room who appeared to be the equivalent of a priest. I saw women, who were possessed by spirits, dancing in front of us. Some of them were smoking cigars and the others were drinking alcohol. I remember asking, "If they're possessed by gods then why are they smoking cigars and drinking alcohol?" I didn't get an answer to that question. It was an interesting experience, and I enjoyed the sense of adventure as well as the sound of the bells they used in the music.

One thing I wanted to do in Brazil was Ayahuasca but because of a commitment I had, I was unable to do it. Bizarrely, I felt like I had the purging experience on the day before I was due to leave. I was walking back to my hostel after lunch, and I started to get hives. When I got into my empty hostel room, I couldn't find my antihistamines and fainted, twice. I managed to call reception to ask for help and right after, I purged. My lovely roommates ended up cleaning up the mess, and I was carried to another room to rest. I was worried about whether I would be able to fly home the next day.

The next day, I was feeling slightly better and managed to drag myself to the airport. I was worried whether they would let me board my flight and I was surprised and disappointed when they told me that my flight had been cancelled and I was due to fly the next day. They put me in a hotel in the town centre, which allowed me to go see the Christ the Redeemer statue, which was the one thing I didn't manage to do. It was like a spiritual experience for me, and I embraced the opportunity as a metaphor to go there and redeem whatever I wanted to about my life.

When I left Brazil and came back home, I felt like I'd become lighter, and I had let go of a lot of attachments that I had from the past. I felt free, illuminated, and spacious inside. It was a powerful experience. When I came back, my manifestation powers were so strong. I entered a competition and won two free tickets to the National Geographic Food Festival. I declared I would do a TEDx talk, and I made it happen within six months. I said I wanted a contract that would pay me a certain amount and I got that. It was crazy.

My three tips for an aspiring solo female traveller:

1. Get clear with yourself about *why* you want to travel solo. Quite often, your reason is a great thing to reflect on when you start to doubt your decision to travel solo due to fear. It can also help you plan the experiences you want.
2. Get clear on *how* you want to travel and your comfort level. You may choose a destination and book the first few nights' accommodations, then take it from there. You may prefer to join a tour group because you'd feel safer. You may choose to stay in nice hotels but prefer to take the bus around.
3. Be prepared and trust yourself. Ensure you *research* the location to respect local cultures and avoid dodgy areas. Once you've done this, know that you're never alone and that there are generous people in all destinations that want to know you and help you if you're in trouble.

Meet Vaishali Patel, a transformation expert empowering people to discover their true selves and embrace their voice. Invited to speak at TEDx, she delves into the power of creative expression for self-awareness and healing. With certifications as a Life Coach, NLP Practitioner, and Reiki Master, along with her Art and Dance Therapy enthusiasm, Vaishali brings nearly two decades of corporate marketing and communication leadership to her coaching. She guides individuals in mastering public speaking while her book, Solo Explorers, empowers women to embrace solo travel and unleash their full potential. Join her in a journey of self-discovery and personal growth.

Website: www.solo-explorers.com
Instagram: @solo.explorers
Facebook: vaishaliauthor

Website: www.vaishali-patel.com
Instagram: @vaishali_tedx

CELEBRATE MY LIFE

Kharytia Bilash

I felt like a failure, again. My husband and I had divorced and then two years later, my successful musical theatre career came to an end when I lost my voice. It wasn't anything health related, I just couldn't sing anymore. It had been such a huge part of my identity. I started working in restaurants and then for a fashion distributor and slowly, I could feel just how unhappy I was with myself.

One day, I thought about having a luxurious trip to live the life that I dreamed of, where I would shop and not care about the price, and then commit suicide. I would max out my credit card, and then that was going to be it. I started imagining how I would do it. It made me feel good for a while.

After a while, however, I realized that I don't want to leave my family with the burden of clearing my debts. I was trying to find how I could do this without my family being impacted and I didn't want to type it into Google because then people would find out. I tried to ask my mother covertly, but being my mother, she picked up on this. She asked, "How can I help you?" I remember thinking, *If I'm going to plan this beautiful, amazing trip, then maybe, I'm probably not going to want to leave the world at the end, I'm probably going to want to keep living.*

I changed my mind, and I sought help from energy healers and a coach. Then my mother said, "I will pay for your plane fare to get there and then you've got to cover the rest." I had worked through all my sadness and decided I would travel to celebrate my life.

I'd been obsessed with Latin cultures all my life and decided I would go to Spain. To ease me into travelling by myself, I flew to Bordeaux in the south of France, where my godmother and her husband lived. From there, I would take the bus to Spain. I remember feeling very lucky. Growing up, I travelled a lot. I'd been to Africa, South America, and most of Europe, but I'd never been to Spain.

I was excited and a little nervous as it had been a long time since I had travelled. I was somewhat fragile in my perception of myself at the beginning, but the trip gave me some motivation to finally do what I wanted. In the past, I would go to the places that my parents insisted on or because the guy I was dating at the time wanted to go. This time, it was where I wanted to go. This had a profound impact on me; it inspired me to start accepting myself and not feel like I had to apologise for my choices and my desires.

Ryanair at the time was having a huge sale and I managed to get a few flights between cities in Spain for 10 euros. I felt empowered. I was very mindful of not having a bag that was too big because I love fashion and I want to look good, but the whole point of this trip was to feel good.

I was excited and nervous when I arrived in France. Seeing my godmother and her husband at the airport made me feel relaxed and I felt at ease going shopping to buy a few bits as some of my belongings hadn't arrived due to a broken zip on my suitcase. At this point, I had been practising my Spanish but not my French, and I was mixing up a lot of the vocabulary, but I got by. My Godmother was wonderfully sweet and just so authentically human. It touched me and made me think that there was hope.

From that point on, I felt really good about the trip. When they walked me to the bus to go to Spain, I was so scared, because from this point on, I didn't know anyone, and I was by myself. I had a flashback of a trip where I was on a night train from Budapest to Ukraine during the Soviet Union times, and I was abruptly woken up with lights being shined into my eyes to make sure that they matched my passport photo. I didn't let the fear stop me, though. With where I was in my life, I had no expectations and nothing to lose. That was probably the most beautiful thing, I was just so excited to be there.

There were little angels everywhere I went. There's something about surrendering to life that way where an unforeseeable force holds you. Sometimes, I would wonder into a rough part of town without realising and suddenly, a young guy would start to walk with me. At first, I was suspicious about their intentions, but it was always a nice conversation to my destination. People would ask me where I came from and if I walked by myself and they showed great relief when I told them that someone had walked me there. They were concerned because there was a high level of crime that happened in that area. I was touched by the amount of care shown to me, a stranger that barely speaks the language. The amount of responsibility these local people took over me was touching and I wanted to pay that forward whenever I could.

I was walking through the aquarium in Valencia and so many people engaged with me, not from a place of pity because I was alone, but more from complete interest. I felt so giddy and joyful and quite unaware of being alone. I felt so engaged and empowered. I had an epiphany that we were all equal and there was this beautiful unity amongst us as if we were all travellers and it didn't matter where we were from, we were all there for the same reason.

I felt a real ease connecting with people. I was staying in a four-person hostel in Madrid and one morning, I woke up and two of the girls were asleep and one girl was awake. We started talking quietly and I told her that I'm going to the biggest flea market in Europe and invited her to come. We took off for this flea market and I didn't even know her name. She helped me barter because she lives in Mexico and spoke fluent Spanish. She bought something and didn't have the right change, so I handed her some money. Later, we went to get food and she offered to pay and told me to get dinner and we were so easy about it.

I spent six hours with this girl, and we paid for each other's food and some of our purchases and I only found out later that her name was Jenny. I saw that we're all the same. We just want to belong, to be seen, to be recognised, and to be able to share ourselves, openly; and ironically, that's easy to do with a stranger sometimes.

There was this one time when I was waiting to get on the train to go to the airport in Malaga to fly to Barcelona. I met an older Irish gentleman, and we started chatting and by the end of the conversation, he'd told me about all four of his sons, and that he thought I would be a good match for the youngest three as the first one was already married. He invited me to visit his town and said, "Just show up and ask for us. You don't need my number; people will send you to us." I thought this was so beautiful.

I felt there is a place for me in this world and the world wants me here, even if sometimes, I don't feel it. It made me aware of the skills that I have.

This trip gave me clarity and the tools to recognise what it was that I wanted my life to be about, and what I wanted my relationships to be like. I got clear on the morals and ethics I wanted to live by and how I wanted to live. Once that became clear, it suddenly felt like my life had so many possibilities that I never considered.

I'm an actor and I've always done acting and had been considering going into the film industry. I didn't feel like I was getting a lot of success. It was a difficult time because I had so much success with musical theatre. I dreamt of creating a film that inspired people to see and consider possibilities and to recognise how wonderful they are. Often what people seek, they already are, they just aren't allowing themselves to be it. I discovered this about myself on the trip. People who barely knew me would tell me that I would be amazing at that, and I was wondering how they knew — and they just knew.

In acting, any layer of censorship, reservation, or insecurity shows up as bad acting on camera. Having encountered genuine people on my travels, I was able to recognise the meaning of authenticity. Because I had nothing to lose, I felt myself being genuine and authentic on my travels. I was confident and this was reflected in my photos. A friend told me that I looked different and that my confidence shows in my looks. This brought the importance of authenticity to the forefront for me.

My three tips for an aspiring solo female traveller:

1. When in doubt, project confidence because the better you feel about yourself, the more people will be drawn to you, and they are more likely to either help or want to be with you.
2. Be unapologetic about your choices; do what you want.
3. Trust. I think that there's a bit of fear when travelling, especially as a solo woman. But there was always an angel in the form of some usually kind man who didn't necessarily come to my rescue but was there to ensure that I was safe.

LET'S NOT PLAY SMALL

Dawn Ritter-Fischer

These last six years have been about breaking out of a self-identity of what I call 'playing small.' It's why I now personalize all my creative writing with the hashtag #letsnotplaysmall. This is my daily reminder to imagine a bigger life, choose growth options whenever possible, look closer at the world around me, and love harder.

I believe that many women get stuck and feel like their life is mundane, uncentered, and boring. We ask ourselves, "Is this it?" They become unsure how to move forward, not even realizing that the movement they likely crave must come from within. For me, this internal growth started after my divorce. I'd realized during that phase of my life that I really had no idea how to be vulnerable with myself or others and it was holding me back from living the life I'd imagined. I decided to change that.

I decided to develop a different self-identity that would allow me to have more vitality, creativity, and human connection. You see, from the outside, I had it all. The successful career, beautiful family, house, and travel, but beneath all that was an introvert incapable of seeing more, being more, and doing more.

My daughter got me involved in yoga during the divorce. The mental and physical "changes" that came as a result of my yoga practice provided the impetus that started my #letsnotplaysmall attitude. A quiet confidence was brewing beneath the surface. I started being more vulnerable with people in my life by having intimate and authentic conversations. Slowly, I began seeing little snippets of the woman I had visualized, vital and full of stories. But the biggest lesson I learned was that to continue realizing these traits and growing into the woman I wanted to become, I was going to have to get comfortable with being uncomfortable.

I'd always loved to travel, so I challenged myself to build even more confidence and assurance in my capabilities by purposefully travelling solo. It scared the hell out of me. I also chose to become scuba certified on that first solo travel trip because that too scared the hell out of me. In 2015, I took myself to Belize and became scuba certified. I arrived terrified and left Belize feeling brave and powerful. That first trip started the trajectory that would eventually become a full-time nomadic lifestyle. It was also my first foray into my art, healing through my writing, and evolving into the confident, never say never woman I am today because of my travels.

When I returned to the US from Belize, I made a life-changing decision to do something else that was super uncomfortable, majorly challenging, and a little crazy. I decided to move from Wisconsin to Texas. Throughout the following year, I sold my house, moved into a smaller rental, organized paperwork with my company for a transfer and mentally manifested the life I would build for myself in Texas. I realized then that I'd created a monster in myself with this craving for change, challenge, and physical/ emotional discomfort. The exact things I'd lived my entire life avoiding.

I moved to Texas in 2015, completely on my own, bought a house for the first time on my own, began dating again (wildly uncomfortable), and travelled as often as possible. During my travels to Vietnam and Morocco, I discovered my creative side. I'd never considered myself a creative person but here I was, writing about all the things I was feeling and experiencing. I challenged myself to develop what I called #personaday. I'd write stories about the people I met on my travels. For an introverted person, getting up the nerve to start those conversations was life-altering. I learned people love to share their stories and listening to them helped me get outside of myself a bit too. The thought of sharing my musings with anyone was terrifying but this was also growth I craved, so I took the leap and began sharing my stories on social media.

By the time the end of 2018 rolled around, I made the difficult decision to take early retirement from my company when it was offered and decided to travel full-time; I couldn't anymore. My biggest fear by now was living a normal conventional life. This was my best shot. I rented out my home in Texas, gifted 95% of my belongings, and headed to South America. First up in this nomadic life were Chile and Argentina. I also spent months living on a sailboat in the Caribbean. I went to Europe and walked 800 miles across Spain, then on to Portugal, Ireland, and the UK. The more I moved about that first year, the more addicted to this life I became. I've never regretted this decision. The more I do it, the more powerful I feel and the more I learn who I am.

It's not always easy. I've had crazy adventures on bus trips and trains where I've completely missed my stops, and I've been lost in places that made me wonder just for a moment, *Why am I doing this???*

A pivotal moment in my travels:

India was one of the most inspiring yet frustrating countries of my travels. I smile when I think back about my time there and everything that transpired. I was putting on my brave hat to go there on my own to begin with. I remember an eight-hour ride from Munnar to Mysuru, where there were three of us crammed on a seat for two and it was very hot on the bus. The windows were opaque with red dust. Some were open and some were closed. As I sat there, one of my flip-flop went sliding across the floor as the bus turned around yet another mountainous curve. It was hot. I was miserable and a little frightened by the reckless manner in which the driver was taking us through the mountains. Oddly enough, I'd just written and shared with some friends how much I was loving my time in India. I was bragging about how I was doing so well manoeuvring the culture. As I sat there on that bus wondering how I was going to get my flip-flop back at some point, I thought to myself, *How do you like it now?*

When I arrived at my hostel at 3am, it was still closed. I dejectedly went around back to the gardens of the hostel where it felt safe. I remember thinking about the previous few weeks and remembering the good as well as the bad I'd experienced thus far in India. The weird vibes at the ashram, the kind couple I'd met at my first homestay in Kerala that I remain in contact with today, and the myriad of people I met from all walks of life in Munnar. I remember thinking, *This is exactly why I travel. The past two days were scary, and I'm exhausted, but I'm safe. The hostel will open in a couple of hours, and I'll continue with this simple, yet often complicated challenging life I purposefully chose and that I've come to love so much. This is not playing small.*

A significant moment in my travels was when I was in Vietnam. A creative side of me was emerging from this first fully solo trip. It was when I began to feel the nudge to write. Not typical stories, but stories of pain, loss, and evolving, human connection. Whatever came up in my emotions or through the people I forced myself to engage with. I remember thinking, *What if I could just do this full-time?* I was still working at the time, and it was probably when the nomadic life seed was planted in my subconscious. My creative side was developing and pushing through the business persona, and I loved it. I believe that trip to Vietnam was when I started manifesting this unconventional life I'm living currently.

I don't have a home base, usually, I'm out of the US travelling in one country or another. Sometimes for months at a time. Moving from place to place typically every seven days or so. Sometimes, I do group tours but most of the time, I'm on my own. I am very conscious about safety as a solo traveller. When I arrive in a new place, I always try to at least know where I'm going or am going to stay for a couple of days just to get the lay of the land.

There were some places that I chose to travel to at which friends and family raised their eyebrows. Concerned typically for my safety. But now, after three years of this, through a pandemic, across six continents, I'm feeling confident with my abilities. My kids and family are always encouraging and asking what's next. I feel like my adopted lifestyle at age 57 showed my grown son and daughter that you can make your life your own, choose another path, and become a better version of yourself, at any age. I'm permitting my grown children to live their life on their terms.

Finances

The first few years after my early retirement at 57, I lived on my savings. I'd been regularly saving because I thought I was going to buy another house to use as an investment property. The universe had other ideas. When I had the opportunity for early retirement, I had plenty of money saved to finance a few years of nomadic travel. It was not a decision I made lightly, and I listed out all the pros and cons, creatively figuring out how I could travel like this for a long time very frugally. I got a TEFL certification so I could teach English if I wanted to make money along the way. I joined a housesitting website so I could have free accommodation along the way. I sorted all the expenses I thought I would incur and determined I could live this way, travelling regularly for less than it would cost me to live at home. Right now, I'm living on around $40,000 a year and I'm able to draw on my pension to support my lifestyle, but I still travel very frugally.

I'm writing a book of my own to encourage and inspire women to live the life they desire. To play bigger and step out of the conventional life and into something exciting, demanding, challenging and joyous. Whatever that means to them. I share how I created this lifestyle, my travel stories from all over the world, and the valuable life lessons I've learned along the way. How I'm stronger than I'd ever imagined, more creative than I ever realized and significantly more open-minded than I was three years ago when I started. And those are the things of a good life.

A decision that I'll never regret on my travels.

I made myself crazy for a week before I went to Antarctica. It was not originally in my travel plans when I went to Argentina to hike Patagonia. I met a young woman on a cargo ship I was on, alongside animals, cars, and cargo on the lower deck, and she was headed to Ushuaia, Argentina to board a vessel to Antarctica. I remember thinking, *How cool is that?* I also remember thinking, *That's a trip that other people get to do. Not people like me.* The financial cost was exorbitant for my budget. But the closer I got to Ushuaia, the more I had this niggling idea in the back of my mind: *What if I go to Antarctica??*

After weighing all the financial considerations and thinking a lot about the cost, I decided to leave it up to the universe. When I arrived in Ushuaia in March 2019, it was the last week for vessels to leave for Antarctica. I decided if I can get on a ship because I'd be booking very last minute, it would be a sign that I was supposed to go.

The day I arrived, I went to all the travel agencies in town and told them, if you can get me on a ship, I can be ready to go within 30 minutes, just call or email me. The days went by, and I thought it wasn't going to happen, then one of the agencies contacted me. I was the last guest to book on the last vessel to leave for Antarctica that year. I'd have a roommate I didn't know, but my fate was sealed. I was going to Antarctica. It was the first time that I remember thinking, *You have the power to make other dreams come true as well.* What a boost for my self-confidence that trip was. This was wilder than my wildest dreams for my travels and I will never regret that decision.

All of this I've shared today wouldn't have happened if I'd just continued living my little conventional life in Texas. Maybe I'd have travelled on a couple of trips a year while continuing a career that never did serve me, but I wouldn't have grown emotionally and spiritually. I wouldn't have learned how much more I have to offer the world, how to serve and inspire other women just by living this unconventional, beautiful life (#letsnotplaysmall).

My three tips for an aspiring solo female traveller:

1. Allow yourself the luxury of rest days. Days where you will sip coffee at a nearby cafe and just watch the world go by. There is no other place you need to be except here at this moment. Breathe.
2. Build a routine of self-care into your travel. Breathing exercises, meditation, yoga, whatever it is, these physical and mental resets offer up a reprieve for the nervous system so necessary for truly seeing the world around you, making better decisions, and opening the heart to the connections that will surely come.
3. Wear clothing with lots of pockets. You'll thank me for it later.

Vaishali Patel

Dawn Ritter Fischer is an American writer, social media contributor, and full-time solo nomadic traveller. In 2019, at age 57, she left behind a conventional life to travel the world and purposefully craft a life full of experiences instead of things. She's currently writing her 1st first travel memoir. #letsnotplaysmall

Website: www.letsnotplaysmall.com
Instagram: @letsnotplaysmall
Facebook: Dawn Ritter Fischer

MEETING MYSELF POST-RETIREMENT

Daeyoung Kim

After serving my organisation for 20 years, I took retirement at the end of October 2018. I was coming out of life-long guaranteed stability to a new chapter in my life where I had no safety net. It was new for me not to be working. I was afraid of retirement and was experiencing self-doubt about what to do next.

In February 2019, I was deep in depression, and I was struggling. I heard about a term called self-compassion and meditation, which I was unaware of as a working professional woman in Korea. I thought I was strong and fearless and didn't need meditation in my life. I realised that I didn't know anything about meditation, and it was something I wanted to explore. I spent hours researching the topic and came across a training, which was due to start in two weeks in Ho Chi Min City. This was a city that I had never imagined travelling to.

I was feeling conflicted. My mind was full of fearful thoughts and my heart was telling me to go. I vividly remember that night when I made the sudden decision to go. I was overwhelmed with different emotions, feeling down and depressed because I had not found what I wanted to do during my retirement. What I had was a strong desire for change.

I'd travelled for business in Korea and abroad all the time. I was well-connected, and I always had somebody at my arrival point. All my business travels were well organized without any ambiguity. At the beginning of my retirement, I took my first solo travel trip at the age of 48. I was scared. I managed to convince my family, despite their fear and worries, that I needed to do this and needed to take on this challenge.

It was a challenge from the day I arrived. The city was beautiful and big despite the country being in a poor situation. The taxi, which took me from the airport to the hotel, was not in a good condition and I was scared on the drive there. I saw families put their children in front of them on a bike/motorbike or in a bag. Sometimes a bike would hold the whole family. All of a sudden, the driver said we'd arrived at my destination, and he pointed to a hotel. I was amazed because the hotel was really beautiful in comparison to the roads and the local markets we drove through.

Ho Chi Min City was a very busy city; I could not figure out where to walk as a pedestrian. I got lost several times. I wasn't able to work out how to use the public transportation system, so I walked from my hotel to the training venue every morning. The roads were beautiful, lined with trees and flowers. I saw that Vietnamese women and men ride their bicycles all the time.

One day, one of my classmates offered to pick me up with her bike from my hotel. I was afraid because I had never sat on a bike before. She suggested that I sit behind her, and I was reluctant at first and told her that I was very heavy. We gave it a try, nonetheless, and we ended up falling off the bike. We couldn't stop laughing. I tried it and I failed, and it was okay because at least I tried it for the first time.

I noticed that I was starting to have compassion for myself. The course was working. It was full of love, compassion, and consideration and took place in the middle of a beautiful garden. In Korea, I worked in public service where training is formal. In Ho Chi Minh city, everything was natural and in flow. The scenery, sounds, smells, and breeze. Everything made me smile and relax.

During the training, my trainer told us that if we needed a nap during the training, we were allowed to take one, as our health and well-being was the most important thing. I thought he was joking until I saw that some participants were lying down and sleeping! They even put their feet on a chair while sleeping in the class. In Korea, that kind of self-care behaviour is unseen. I had a bit of culture shock. On the other side of the globe, people behave differently. I was surprised by how open-minded all the participants were to talk about sad childhood memories. I was impressed to see everyone supporting each other.

Self-compassion was the biggest thing I learnt through the training I attended. In Korea, compassion doesn't form part of our culture. I would go as far as to say that we don't even know the meaning of compassion. Self-compassion is based on equality and equity. Korean culture is very hierarchical, and we confuse sympathy and empathy. With that in mind, I chose to pursue a career to contribute to creating a cultural transformation in Korea, with compassion as one of the core values that I share with my clients and people.

I started a new phase of my life after this solo trip to Vietnam. I learned that fear is a part of myself, it will always be there with me, and that is ok. I now recommend solo travel for people like me who are thinking about a career change, because they can discover and meet themselves throughout the journey. I saw that I could be an advocate for myself in Korean culture.

My three tips for an aspiring solo female traveller:

1. Listen to your inner whispering and follow your heart.
2. Allow yourself to explore — not to succeed or to fail.
3. Enjoy being there.

Daeyoung is an igniter who helps people to unlearn their culture and empowers people to reclaim their gifts. She is an EQ practitioner, certified coach, and educator. She believes that we thrive via international exchange.

Linkedin: daeyoung-kim-08198010b

TRUSTING MYSELF IN THE UNKNOWN

Jennifer Morhaime

I was in my mid-20s when I went to Europe for the first time. I desperately needed a change and had always wanted to go to Europe. I had a few friends that were living abroad at the time and decided it was time to branch out and go over to visit, and at the same time, to figure out what my next plan in life was. I was lucky to be in a job where I had the flexibility to take off for three weeks to go live out this adventure.

I had planned to go to Italy first because of the connection to my grandfather being Italian and my minor in college was Italian studies. I never looked at a map to get around and I never got lost. I had this sense that my grandfather was with me telling me where to go, even though he wasn't there. I felt so calm navigating myself in an unknown yet familiar territory. It was as if I was at home. Italy was exactly what I dreamed it would be. The food, the people, the smells, the wine, the art, the music, and the gelato.

Italy was a great initial destination, a bit of a buffer before I got to London. London was more unfamiliar, even though I was staying with friends for free. They worked during the day and that's when I would go on adventures of my own around London. I wanted to go to London because I wanted to go to a place where I understood the language. I further expanded my ability to get around. Navigating the tube was a big deal for me because I've had major anxiety trying to navigate the subway system in New York and Chicago. It was a big step for me to do things on my own, and I learnt that I can navigate new places and find things on my own without needing somebody to rely on. Seeing how organized the tube was made my fear drift away. Navigating the tube solidified my confidence and self-awareness.

On my way to Germany, my flight to Munich from London got diverted in the middle of the night, due to an electrical issue, to Linz, Austria. From there, they put us on a bus to Munich. I had to try and figure out how to contact my friend who I was visiting, without using Wi-Fi, using my cell phone. There was only one payphone in the airport too. I was uncomfortable but I had to trust other people on the plane to translate what the guides were saying because they were speaking in German. I had to surrender all doubt and trust that whatever somebody was telling me was happening.

I listened to the person that was sitting next to me on the bus translate, and when we got to Munich, he helped me work out how to get a bus to where I needed to go. All the buses stopped as it was 3am and I was supposed to get in at 10pm. I didn't get into my friend's apartment until 6am. When I came by her apartment, my friend was standing outside her apartment, at the exact time that I pulled up in the bus. She said, "I just had this sense that I needed to wake up and check to see if you were out front." It was one of those crazy moments, but my previous self would have just been crying and upset. It showed how much strength I have and that even in scary situations, I can still push through.

I feel like travel has given me independence and confidence that I can do anything. Small things that might seem scary, going into them, and developing the mindset that if I just jump into it, I'll succeed and move forward. That takes the fear out of the unknown. Knowing that I can do anything I set my mind to. I met people along the way that offered to help and there were people there to support me, even though I was on my own.

After I returned home, I had the urge to go back. I fell in love with Europe and felt like it was part of me and where I was supposed to be. I told my parents that I want to move there. They kept telling me that it was wonderful because it was a vacation and living there may not be the same. I needed to explore this, and so I planned another trip for the following year. I had made a friend in Italy, who offered to let me come stay with him. I went and stayed with him so that I could immerse myself and see what living in Florence would feel like.

After a while, I decided that I needed to face my fears back at home versus running from them and decided not to move to Europe. I came back home and faced my fears, to see what life could be like if I made some changes. The fear I was running from was that I wasn't going to find a friend or a partner in life. I was feeling like I was being left behind by a lot of my friends, and I was also in a job that didn't warrant any social life. I was dating continuously and trying to meet people but struggling to be social because I just didn't have anybody to bounce ideas off at work. I was feeling lost.

I had a lot of trust issues about relationships, and I threw those out the window when I was travelling. I met great people, had some experiences, broke down some of my walls, and was a free bird. I came back and it gave me a different self-confidence. I was able to open up and trust people a little bit more. Travel was able to open some doors and relationships. I had one relationship right after the second trip, which lasted about a year and then that led me to my now husband.

Through solo travel, I gained confidence. I never thought that I would be somebody that would be on the road having to navigate new parts of a country by myself. I now apply that to my job when I go to a new state for customers; it set me up for success in my role and my job now. The confidence I built navigating countries has just shaped the fact that I know where I'm going and, if I take a wrong turn, I'll be okay. I learned to trust myself in the space of the unknown and that helped manage my anxiety.

Trusting myself in the unknown during my travels helped me manage some of the anxiety I felt when writing a self-help book. It has helped me create adventures in my children's book series, *Effie's Adventures,* too. Each time Effie meets a new friend, I draw those emotions from meeting new people on my travels.

Travel and mastering navigation have helped me feel more confident in life. It has helped me realize that I can do the job that I'm in now because I had shied away from sales jobs that included travel. I just didn't feel comfortable travelling alone, but now I feel confident and know that I'm safe and there are always a lot of ways to support myself, even if I'm by myself.

My three tips for an aspiring solo female traveller:

1. Just do it.
2. Plan and figure out what you want to see and do and make a list before you go. When you get there, don't worry if you don't reach your plan. Scratch off what you can but do what you want and enjoy the moment. One of the things I did for both trips was create my itinerary, and I broke it down by day, but then when I got there, I used it as a guide to help me know where I want to go. I did my research so that I would feel comfortable knowing where to go and what to do; I had all the little pocket maps ready to go and everything. That helped me navigate, and let go of my fears, because I knew the research and I knew what I was getting myself into.
3. On the other side of fear is success! Put yourself out there and take a risk, you will be surprised by what you find out about yourself and others. Let the fear go and drink in the freedom of being alive.

Jennifer is a published children's book author, top sales manager covering multiple states and national accounts, wife and mother of 2 young boys. Traveling, creating and sharing life experiences are a true passion and lifelong dream.

Website: www.jmorhaimebooks.com
Instagram: @effies_books

FOREVER DARING, EXPLORING, AND CURIOUS

Jennifer Lin

Who knew that joining a youth programme for China Youth Corps, which aims to entice the youth of society to give back to the community, would open my eyes to a whole other side of life! Before then, I was a simple girl, living a simple life. I volunteered on a programme that introduced Taiwan to foreign students to learn about new cultures. I had no idea what awaited me. I learnt about sex and rock and roll, and it was the first time I smoked weed. I experienced what LSD was like and was having sex much more freely, without the intention of getting married. It was a mind-opener and I wanted to experience more of that.

I got my opportunity in the summer of 1980 when I accepted a scholarship to learn German at the University of Vienna. At the time, I was in my senior year of college at the National Taiwan University.

Vienna was the ultimate in sophistication, romance, and culture for me. I was surprised that I could casually stroll in and listen to the music at the opera house. For the entire week, I visited the museum daily and would stand there for hours looking at various artefacts. I was mesmerised by the culture and the artistic achievements of various artists.

Two weeks into my month-long stay in Vienna, I decided to visit the rest of Europe. I was surprised to learn that I couldn't travel freely around Europe because of my Chinese passport. The only country I could travel to without a visa was the Vatican. I realised that I had to apply for a visa in advance to travel anywhere in Europe, with the possibility that it could be rejected because of my passport. That's when it dawned on me that politics could be a huge hindrance to free travel and exploring the world.

Despite the visa situation, I managed to travel to Germany, Austria, Italy, Belgium, UK, and France for eight weeks.

There were moments when I felt scared when travelling in Italy. I was an Asian woman travelling on my own, which was rare 40 years ago, and I attracted much male attention. Travelling on my own, at a time when most Asian women didn't, could be seen as dangerous and unsafe. But I was too daring and fearless to entertain ideas like that.

On some level, it was freeing. Men would strike up a conversation and flirt with me, and it was a flattering experience. However, on this one occasion, there were a couple of youngsters following me around while I was shopping. I was trying on some clothes in the changing room when suddenly, one of the men came into the changing room and started to get very physical. It didn't matter how scared I was or how sexually pleasing it was, I was uncomfortable, and I didn't know what to do. I remembered that the right thing to do by my cultural upbringing was to be shy and try to get out of the situation as quickly as I could without being confrontational and screaming, "Don't touch me again without my consent!" Quite a large cultural burden that I carry is that we're taught to never say no. Even if there's something that you don't like, you are expected to be polite and avoid the situation.

This experience taught me that those cultural expectations influenced my behaviour in this situation, leading to a negative impact on my safety and comfort. However, I learned the importance of speaking up and saying no when I don't wish to give my consent or feel my boundaries are being crossed. It's okay to assert myself and protect my well-being.

Dealing with the hurdles and obstacles I faced with visas, I realised that I can be unreasonable and unstoppable. I had faced the unknown and I got through the obstacles and from this point on, the options and the possibilities that opened were mind-blowing. I found myself making a declaration that I will be forever daring, exploring, and curious.

My new determination would make my friends worry. I remember walking freely through areas of Belgium that were considered not safe, and my friends being surprised. The thing is, I felt a new faith in humanity when walking alone, that people would not take advantage of me but help me. That still prevails in my life now. I have no fear of asking for help with directions and people would help me and sometimes accompany me. Not having a predetermined judgement of people's intentions enabled me to travel freely.

Being able to freely travel somewhere I liked because I was drawn by the beauty of a place was new for me. Before that, I was restricted in where I could travel because of diplomatic relations between Taiwan and other countries as well as social restrictions back then for women. I was one of the few women that went travelling by myself, as many women from Taiwan would join organised group tours. I'm grateful that I can travel wherever I like now freely and expand my horizons.

During a two-week holiday in the UK in 2016, I made a declaration that London would be my next place of residency and property investment would be my next career. That European trip over the summer had planted seeds of being daring and unreasonable. I finally moved to London and started my property investment business in December 2019.

My three tips for an aspiring solo female traveller:

1. Planning well is crucial for successful solo travel; research the destinations you want to visit, create a flexible itinerary, and book accommodation in advance. Stick to a realistic budget to manage expenses effectively throughout your trip.
2. When choosing where to go, take into account your physical capabilities to ensure a comfortable and enjoyable journey. Opt for destinations that align with your interests and offer activities suitable for your fitness level. Additionally, prioritise

safety by checking travel advisories and avoiding areas with security risks.

3. Embrace the solo travel experience with an open and friendly attitude; smile and engage with locals and fellow travellers alike to build connections and make friends from different cultures. Being approachable and sociable can enrich your journey, leading to memorable interactions and shared experiences.

Jennifer Lin Shay is the Managing Director of Marvel Group. She embarked on her 2nd professional career in the UK property market as an investor at the advanced age of 58 after nearly two decades in public relations/corporate communications in Asia.

She founded Marvel Success (Worldwide) Ltd., a property investment company when she first relocated to the UK in 2016. With over two decades of experience, an innate business acumen, analytical insight and a disciplined work ethic, and on top of assembling nearly £5M assets for herself, Jen established Marvel Success to help Hong Kong and Asian investors achieve their strategic property investment goals, by building a network of trusted UK property Deal Sourcers.

Jen obtained her master's degree in Corporate Communication from the Chinese University of Hong Kong in 2005 and a BSc in Botany from the prestigious National Taiwan University in 1981.

Website: www.marvelsuccess.co.uk

A JOURNEY INTO THE UNKNOWN

Sharon Wilson

The real value in learning is doing something by yourself, and I was on a path to grow and expand. It was time to come out of my comfort zone, so I decided to organise a solo travel trip myself. I am not a natural planner, so historically, my friends or family usually organised our travels and I just turned up and enjoyed the experience.

One of my main concerns was that I am directionally challenged and if I were to go into a maze, I would probably not find my way out until the following day. Even when I'm driving a car, I can go around a roundabout a few times just to make sure I find my bearings. Although Sat-Navs help to a certain degree, I still find myself lost. This time, however, I chose to organise the whole trip by myself and navigate the journey — travelling on buses rather than taking taxis — to stretch myself and expand my knowledge.

Because I love creativity and spontaneity, I wanted to find a fun way to do this. So, I put all the letters of the alphabet into a hat and decided to choose a destination based on the letter I pulled out. After giving the hat a good shake, I picked the letter 'N.' The plan was to take a five-day break and use a low-cost airline. I went onto the EasyJet website and told myself that the first place that came up with the letter N was the destination I was going to. It was Naples in Italy! I was excited and looking forward to my solo travel adventure. Before my trip, I looked online for things I could do in Naples and printed out the maps and locations to refer to.

When I arrived in Naples, I got onto a packed bus with my suitcase and managed to find a seat. It was very busy, and I was looking out for the bus stops and thinking, *This is going well.* But I soon realised that I may have missed my stop as I was distracted by watching the many people that got on and off the bus as well as the sights outside.

I remained calm as I had a feeling that my hotel was nearby but, at this point, I needed to ask someone for help. I turned my attention to the crowded bus and could hear people engaged in conversations in heavy Italian. I saw this as an additional challenge and was getting concerned as the bus kept speeding through the winding streets, it was beginning to get dark, and I was getting further and further away from my destination.

I thought about making my way through the crowd to ask the bus driver, but he was talking to people with a heavy Italian accent, and I wasn't sure I wanted to navigate that walk in-between all the people. I turned to the person next to me and pointed to where I was meant to be going on my piece of paper. He didn't speak English but signalled in Italian to me how to stop the bus. He then took my suitcase as I got off the bus and, using sign language, gave me directions to get me on the right path to my hotel. I was pleasantly surprised by the generosity of this stranger — he got off the bus at a stop that wasn't his to help direct me, a stranger, to my hotel.

I noticed that people were kind wherever I went. Whenever I had dinner by myself, the chefs and waiters would come over and talk to me and that made me feel welcome. On a trip to Pompeii, I entered the coach that collected me from my hotel and all I could see were rows of seats with people. As I walked along the aisles, I had to decide where the spaces were and who I was going to sit next to and share this adventure with. I was scanning people's faces and their body language to see who looked friendly or not and ended up sitting next to a man that was travelling alone.

As I usually travelled with friends and family, I had them for company, but I decided that on this trip, I would have to make the effort to get to know new people. I did something I would not usually do, and initiated the conversation, which turned out to be a wonderful and magical experience!

I was glad I did as we ended up doing the whole tour together. He was a former basketball player who worked for L'Oréal and shared some interesting stories. My phone battery was running low, and he ended up taking photos for me that he sent to me afterwards. It was a fabulous adventure where I discovered how kind people can be and that there are also people travelling alone, just like me, whose company I could enjoy and vice versa.

I am a life coach by profession. I am very good at supporting other people to accomplish their goals, aspirations, and dreams, and encouraging them to get outside of their comfort zone as this is where the real growth begins. This trip was a great example of me 'walking my talk' and doing what I challenge my clients to do. As I expanded as a person, I felt my coaching business expand also. Opening my travelling doors paralleled opening new roads for my business. Travel was the catalyst for me to keep going big in all other areas of my life and come out of my comfort zone.

As a result of my travels, I decided to never play small or be comfortable with other people doing everything for me. I think there is a real sense of freedom and empowerment that comes when you do something by yourself that you didn't think you could do. It wasn't always easy as there were challenges to overcome, but it was highly rewarding. Going through the journey, facing the ups and downs, and knowing that I did it myself, enabled me to grow into being a bigger and better version of myself, which I have reflected in my business. As I've grown, it's enabled me to give more to my clients and support them on their journeys to becoming their best selves.

Being in a country where very few people spoke English was challenging and I had relied upon the expectation that most people could communicate in English. That was my assumption, and it was wrong as not many people spoke English in Naples. I remember on one occasion getting on a hop-on hop-off bus and missing my stop. When I got off, it was in a remote place, so there was no one around to ask for directions. I felt a mixture of fear and excitement knowing that I had to get myself out of this. But that is what travelling is all about, taking the road less travelled, dancing with the unknown and doing something you've never done before. When approaching people for help, I found a smile helped as an entry point to break down barriers. People often smiled back, and I then knew I had made a connection. Often, we were both in the same boat, trying to communicate in languages that the other didn't speak or understand. My form of sign language helped me to ask for help and connect with people.

As a tourist visiting Naples, the locals were very humble and treated me kindly when I needed help. It was a fun experience as, sometimes they would invite somebody else over to join the conversation, and we'd use Google Translate to translate the literal words. There was always a way for messages to be understood and plenty of kind strangers and angels around.

I'm very visual and enjoyed taking in the amazing views. At night, I consciously decided that while I was there, I would be present, take in the scenery, live in the moment, and not focus on my fear or concerns about how I was going to get home. Sometimes, whilst taking in the beautiful views, internally, I was thinking, *Oh my gosh, how do I get home from here? It's quite dark.* However, I was clear that I would not take a taxi if I missed a stop as I would have been disappointed with myself because the purpose of my solo travel experience was about figuring things out independently. I would go to a restaurant, relax and sit there, have a drink or some food, and afterwards, ask them for directions to my hotel. I was determined that I was going to enjoy the time and utilise and live every moment.

I did have concerns about dining at a restaurant by myself as I've never done that before, so my insecurities started to come out. I chose to face that fear and started by eating on my own at my hotel. I would go up to the lovely rooftop restaurant and enjoy the ambience. I enjoyed taking the time to sit and observe other people and sit in the moment and connect with people. I had a newfound appreciation of the concept of mindfulness as I could taste my food because I was not in a rush to get anywhere. I was in control of how I spent my time, and it was empowering to know that I could spend it the way I wanted to, on my terms. It was like an adventure as I didn't know whom I was going to meet or whose paths I would cross. People at other tables would smile and start talking to me and sometimes send over glasses of wine. The experiences were expansive and empowering. I now really know what it means when you go on a journey of the unknown for yourself. When things don't go according to plan, that is a journey in itself that takes you on another adventure.

My three tips for an aspiring solo female traveller:

1. Be curious. Approach your trip with childlike wonder and view it as an adventure. Go on an adult adventure without any expectations.
2. Be open and connect with others. Go talk to the people of the country, see what they eat, how they live, and what makes them special, and absorb the culture without comparison or judgement.
3. Be comfortable with the unknown. You never know what's going to happen. You could meet Mr/Miss Right? Or meet someone and have a wonderful friendship or business connection. It's exciting facing the unknown and not knowing the outcome or what's going to happen next in your life's journey.

Sharon Wilson is an award-winning coach with a 25-year career at the London Business School. An advocate for a people-centric culture, she coaches individuals and teams to become their selves at work, study, and life. She also created the Complimentary Kindness initiative.

Website: https://sharonwilson.co.uk

FACING THE FEAR

Twinkle Patel

I had quite a sheltered life up until my trip to India. I was 21 and I had only been on holiday with my family, and up until then, done all the 'right' things a good Indian girl should do. I had never travelled anywhere on my own. When I spoke to my parents about wanting to go on my own to India, they were really surprised as it was out of character for me. I spent a long time convincing my parents to let me go to India after I finished university. I told them that I wanted to connect with my roots and my spiritual side. I had been religious up to that point and felt the desire to grow both spiritually and mentally.

They agreed to let me go when a friend of mine who also led a similar life and shared the same desires wanted to join me. She had lost her dad very early in life and wanted to explore her spiritual side too.

After a few days in India staying with her relatives in Mumbai, I noticed she was acting differently. I experienced hostility towards me and felt she resented me being there and I couldn't understand why. I was feeling lonely in a place surrounded by people that I did not know. I came to realise after that she became jealous of the way her family praised me for the way I looked. She felt like she was compared to me, which made her feel rejected and insecure. We chose to go our separate ways at this point. I was disappointed as we had pre-booked a trip to the south of India together. After much deliberation due to my fears of going on my own, I decided I would do this trip. I was scared but determined to not let my emotions get the best of me.

I felt safe travelling as a solo female traveller in a tour group. I was very conscious about getting sick because I had heard countless stories about people getting extremely sick after eating locally produced food. I had a proper meal the first night at a nice local restaurant in Mysore. After that, I lived on a pack of biscuits and Sprite for morning, lunch and dinner. I just did not want to eat anything else, and it got me through the trip. The tour group in general didn't go to any nice places and stopped at little roadside stalls. There were flies everywhere and I didn't feel comfortable eating there. I sat with the group and joined in on conversations with my biscuits and Sprite.

I spent considerable time visiting temples and walking up endless staircases that would take hours to get to. It was hot and there were no kiosks or water available. I had one bottle of water that I made last for as long as I could. I can recall a moment when I was walking up stone steps in the extreme heat with just my thoughts for conversation. I felt determined to get to the top without passing out and I was alone with no one to support me. It was at that moment that I felt like I was doing this for myself. I was able to reflect, and I asked myself many questions: What is it that I want to do? What do I enjoy? What career will I enter? Will I find a boyfriend? Will I fall in love? Do I want to fall in love? I had endless questions about myself, ultimately exploring who I was and what I wanted. I didn't know the answers to any of the questions. As I took each step, I challenged every thought in my head.

As I was climbing to the top, I was feeling exhausted not just physically but mentally too. When I took my final step and reached the top, something just came over me and I felt this immense blanket of peace. I froze and stared into nothing for a while. That's when I realised that my whole life, I had lived for others, I did what others wanted me to do and never really explored what I wanted or liked. I felt like I had no personality. Little did I know that this moment of self-realisation was going to change my life forever.

Travelling from Goa to Mysore, we stopped off at Hill stations and visited villages where there was a lot of poverty. The people would welcome us into their homes and offer to make us tea. I was very touched that they had little money to feed themselves and their families, yet they would make us feel like celebrities. The kindness and generosity they showed when they had little for themselves was a very humbling experience for me.

Being on my own after a fallout with my friend, despite travelling with a travel group, made me feel vulnerable, scared, and alone. I contemplated booking an early flight home to be with my family who were my comfort and my backbone. But I carried on. I asked the coach driver to stop at internet cafes so I could email my parents to give them updates on where I was. I often found myself breaking down emotionally. My parents were equally concerned about me but didn't want me to give up. They found people I could connect with in India through their network. Overnight, I had a plan arranged for me to stay with uncles and aunties in Mumbai and Gujarat. I realised that I was stronger than I knew myself to be and that I was always held and supported.

Before I went to India, I was timid. I was never the type of person that would approach someone and introduce myself. At university, I made friends with few people and never mixed with the popular crowd. I was self-conscious and afraid to talk and sometimes I didn't know what to say.

During my trip to India, I became a different person, because I had to stand up for myself. There were moments when I was walking down the street and an older man would touch my bum. I was annoyed and would slap their hand away. I would shout my disgust at them in English and people would look over to see what was going on. I would never do that in London. I was never the type of girl to say anything. I would just feel humiliated and let it pass but I was outspoken in India.

There were other moments where I chose to speak up such as when they tried to charge me more because I was a foreigner. I even got playful and tried to convince them that I was from India by using language that I had picked up from my conversations with local people. I would use local conversational language with the taxi driver to make them feel like I knew this place as much as a local person does. It was fun and I was easing into using my voice to get around.

I once complained at a hotel because on the last day of our stay, one of the girls that had gone in for a shower before me saw a guy inside the boiler room, which was connected to our bathroom. We all made a complaint to the female manager who initially denied it and backed her staff. She then made them all line up so we could pick out the culprit. I used my voice to hold them to account for what they did and their standards. The manager was appalled that her staff would act in such a way and was very apologetic. I felt so empowered as I felt I was speaking up for the many women who have encountered any form of discrimination.

Travelling on my own around India gave me the confidence to land a job that I wanted. After sending lots of applications, a top investment bank invited me to an open day. It was my first interview after finishing university and I remember being different; I had self-belief. In many ways, I think the whole experience of travelling and standing up for myself gave me the confidence that I lacked in my childhood. I also felt like I had turned a new corner; I was beginning to enjoy life for me, doing the things that I enjoyed such as trying new cuisines, travelling to new countries, and making new friends.

When I reflect on this trip, what makes me laugh was being mistaken for being an actress by a three-year-old in Goa. As I was walking, a young three-year-old walked up to me and held my hand. We both smiled at each other, and her mother came over to apologise and to say, "She thinks you're an actress." The funny thing is at that point, I was acting my way through life without really knowing who I was inside.

My three tips for an aspiring solo female traveller:

1. Don't give up. Whatever happens and whatever obstacles come your way, persevere because, in the long run, the experience is going to be so much more fulfilling.

2. Embrace it. Embrace everything that you're surrounded by even if at times it can be very overwhelming. Let yourself be open to the experience and this journey.
3. Be true to yourself and stand up for yourself. Let these experiences change you based on your choice to let them change you.

GIVING MYSELF PERMISSION

Melba Palhazy

I was at a stage of my life where I was going through some significant changes. My long-term relationship ended, and my identity was changing now to being a single woman. I needed space to let the old fall apart and create who I was going to be next and what I wanted my life to be about. I had a job, it wasn't exactly nine to five, but it wasn't the kind of free life I wanted. I had the responsibilities of bills, a job, a team, results, and relationships.

One day, I thought, *Oh my God, I know where I want to go.* I have always loved South America and its cultures. But there was this thing about tango that I've always wanted to try and learn. I decided to go to Buenos Aires and learn to tango and practice my Spanish too. The other country on my list was Mexico. I was always drawn to the rich culture, and I had never had the opportunity to go and explore before. I linked the two together and purchased return flights going to Buenos Aires and coming back from Mexico. I turned up in Buenos Aires not having planned anything; I plan everything. I'm the person that has all the details planned out. It was scary and exciting.

I had the intention to immerse myself in the tango scene and wanted to meet with tango dancers. Once I purchased my tickets, I spoke to a few people, and they started connecting me to tango dancers and teachers they knew in Buenos Aires. By the time I landed, I had a tango teacher and a community of tango dancers to connect with. I did not expect to get pulled into the scene so much. The idea was that I'd tango for a few weeks then go to Patagonia and all the other sites in Argentina, and then fly to Mexico City and travel all of Mexico. Little did I know just how powerful the pull of the whole tango scene was.

I've always loved dance and my self-expression is movement. With tango, I got connected to being a woman, to passion, and my feminine essence. I feel Latin women own it much more than women in Europe and it's passed on down generations. People tend to refer to it as sexuality, but I don't think it's specifically sexuality, it's rather the essence of a woman.

When you're younger, you want to be allowed to have your passions and self-expression, but then working life comes at some point or family life, and suddenly, you're supposed to be a certain way, the serious way. Often, especially women, with all the responsibilities we have in life, give up a lot of our self-expression and passions.

Through learning to tango, I discovered much more confidence in myself. In the past, I used to create confidence and self-worth through my work achievements and results. What I found through tango and travelling solo is a more innate feminine confidence. I also got more comfortable leading with my feminine energy rather than my masculine energy. High-performance societies, such as the Western world, are associated with masculine energy more, which is my default style as it's safe. It was transformational to connect to my feminine essence and learn how to handle it, be comfortable with it, and own it.

Tango is such an intense dance, and you have to embrace the closeness with yourself and your partner, which you can't do when you are dealing with overthinking. You're in the way of the dancer within you. So, again, you have to strip away the thoughts until you come to a place of nothing, to allow for vulnerability, especially when you're learning something new. It's kind of uncomfortable and it's a different place, but something becomes available in that vulnerability when you discover something jointly with another human being.

I have now created this whole new life around tango, it has become such a pivotal self-expression that I go back for the season every year.

Travelling around Mexico for six weeks was transformative in another way. There were moments, especially when I was on the plane to Mexico City, when I was thinking about whether I was a bit nuts. Here I was in my 40s and I'd travelled extensively in my 20s as a tour guide, yet I was wondering, *Can I still do it?* Not only that, but I was going to Mexico, which gets such a bad reputation in terms of safety. I discovered there was nothing dangerous about it. I didn't have one single bad experience and I think it's down to how I carried myself and how open I was to connect with people when I travelled, including when flagging down local buses and staying in local Airbnbs. I think I am a bit of a chameleon and like to travel like a local. I think that is one of my strengths, that I don't travel like a tourist.

With the existence of Airbnb, it's much easier to connect in local languages as you can connect directly with the person in their home and have some fantastic conversations that you can't get when you stay in hotels. I remember I was in Oaxaca (pronounced: Wahaca) and I stayed two nights with a woman who was a similar age and was going through something similar. She had just ended a relationship and was telling me about all the complications, and the connection was just amazing. When you speak so deeply and are sharing those moments and what it is to be human, across cultures, it is amazing. I love connecting with local people in their native language and that's why I speak so many languages. How bad or well you speak doesn't matter; I think it gives you a different level of connection.

I did have concerns about being safe and whether my Spanish was good enough. All the personal development work I had done over the years helped me face the fear and concerns and do it anyway. Preparation and planning also helped me to manage my concerns.

I remember coming back with this renewed confidence. People would say to me, "Oh my god, you're so brave," and when I was in the country, the locals would say, "Oh my god, you're travelling on your own." People thought that it was such a great thing to do.

One decision I made because of this trip was to permit myself to fully express my passion — and, you know, maybe this decade might be tango and maybe in the next decade, it will be something else. I'm allowed to change; I'm allowed to change my mind and I'm allowed to have new passions. Another decision was not to apologise anymore for who I am and for my passion.

When I returned to the UK three months later, I changed my whole life. I moved to Cambridge, a city that was much more suitable for the things I enjoyed. My yoga studio is now 15 minutes' walk from my house, and I've been practising daily, if not twice a day. The city centre is 20 minutes away and all the practicalities of aligning with a life of expressing my passions and living my life by design were part of that. Living in a much more pleasant place with my own balcony was part of my creative life. Tango is a big part of my life, and every year, I make space for it, including the logistical practicalities such as saving money and blocking out the calendar, and for those two months or three months, I make it happen. I made it happen for myself because it's important to me and an important part of who I've become. It's become essential that I nurture my passions and nurture this expression of who I am. I don't need to justify it or apologise for it, and everyone around me benefits from it because I am happier and more content.

My three tips for an aspiring solo female traveller:

1. Just do it: Most people on their deathbeds regret the things they didn't do rather than the things they did do. Make the commitment to yourself, "I'm going to do it."
2. Research: Plan and talk to people so you are as prepared as possible. This will help you face your fears.
3. Talk to people: You might be travelling on your own, but you are not on your own. Talk to people. Travel as a local, take interest in people, build your network, and sow your seeds. You never know when these connections will become useful. Create deep connections and networks, which is priceless when you travel.

Melba Palhazy is a multifaceted woman, embodying the essence of movement, mindfulness, and inspiration.

A tango dancer, yogi, passionate traveller and a linguist, she weaves cultural stories through dance and communication. Her love for health, travel and exploration of diverse cultures reflects her deep appreciation for our interconnected world. Melba is a collaborator, facilitator and life coach, guiding others on their journeys of self-discovery.

As a Sustainability Ambassador, she champions holistic practices for a greener world. For her dedication to sustainable communities, Melba was chosen to carry the Olympic Torch at the 2012 London Olympic Games, lighting the way for others to follow.

Melba's life is a testament to the power of passion and purpose, inspiring others to live with intention.

Instagram: @melbapalhazy
Twitter: @MelbaPalhazy

LIMITLESS

Sapna Jawid

I came to the United States as an international student from Pakistan to pursue my higher education. I specifically chose the US for its rich diversity and top-ranked academic opportunities across all disciplines. I didn't realise that it would come with a lot of obstacles. I could legally travel; however, the political landscape at the time made it difficult for international employees and students to travel outside the US and come back. There were some cases where some people weren't allowed to come back to the US even though they had valid visas. It was strongly advised and recommended that international employees do not travel back unless it's a high-priority trip.

I was a full-time student, away from my family and working three jobs. Was this the BIG dream that I came to the US to experience? I was at the lowest point of my life because I felt confined, and I was still not living my authentic life. I grew up wanting to travel the world. I decided that I was through with feeling restricted and I got myself the map of the United States and became defiant that if I couldn't travel out of the country, I was going to travel the entire United States.

My hiking backpack would include my hiking boots, shirts, black pencil heels, and a black pencil skirt. I had just started my job as a higher education professional, so I always carried smart shoes and clothes with me. I took flights on Wednesdays and Thursdays and would be back in the office at 8am on Mondays. In the two years I was there, I ended up travelling to 45 states and 35 national parks in the US on my own. When I finally became a US resident, I was excited that I could extend my passion for travel outside the country.

When it comes to travel, I am a lover of all things less experienced, less touristy, and less accessible. I also seek unusual communities, phenomena, wonders, and tribes. I have always been particularly interested in less travelled regions of Africa and the great Sahara Desert. One day, I came to know about the Eye of Sahara, or the Richat Structure, nestled deep inside the Sahara Desert that fell into north-western Mauritania. There is a great mystery, and some historical geological facts are tied to this place. It is believed that the eye's formation began when the supercontinent Pangaea started to pull apart. The discovery of this place came at a time when international travel was becoming possible for me. Therefore, without much thought, I booked my vacation from work, a drone to capture the aerial shot of the 'Eye,' and tickets to Mauritania. During this trip, a seed was planted and now the world is in my palms.

The turning point of this trip to Africa was when I went to Tanzania because I grew up climbing mountains and I had lost my brother to a mountain. My dad was a mountaineer, and he would take the two of us on summits and high hikes. I spent many a night in national parks and the wilderness, watching the night sky and the milky way. I had bear encounters, stayed alone and endured storms in a tent. Those experiences gave me the skill set to survive in the wilderness.

After summiting Kilimanjaro in Tanzania, I was convinced that the only life I see myself living is the one in which global culture, travel and adventure are in abundance. Sharing my story with the world was important to me, which is why I started a blog and a YouTube channel. I later visited the rare gorillas of Uganda, lived with the tribes of Ethiopia, and found my missing pieces in Kenya.

I try to put my body to some challenge no matter where I go because I'm just hooked on that feeling. Mountains play an important role in my life; they have made me who I am. I love mountains because they make me feel alive unlike anything else and test my body to a point where I feel it's just so impossible. They test my limits and push me. They bring down the nothingness and remind me how little and insignificant I am. How much at the mercy of nature I am. There are many facets that I am, masks that I wear all the time, and mountains pull them off my face and throw me down the drain and remind me, "You are absolutely nothing."

I often feel big and grand in this world that I sometimes don't even realise how incredibly important it is to feel small and the clarity that comes with the understanding that this world does not give a heck whether you live or not. This is when I realise that "Oh my god, my time is so limited." I think mountains do that for me; it's a high that I need to recalibrate myself and my priorities.

Whenever I am faced with a challenge in my daily life, big or small, I think about how I survived climbing mountains and being in the wilderness. Putting myself out there in the wilderness, my mind just went into flight and fight mode so many times. I had situations where I was injured, felt trapped and threatened. In those situations, I learnt how powerful I am, how brave I am, and that I can do anything. To feel self-reliant is arguably the most powerful feeling one could feel, and I am incredibly thankful for all the travel experiences that enable me to be resilient and self-reliant.

I was born privileged, and through my travels, I have come to learn that even though we cannot change the circumstances we are born into, what we can change and must change is our decision of how to use that privilege. Travels put privilege into perspective and allows us to see the realities and perspectives that are quite different and conflicting with ours. Visiting and living with the least contacted tribes of Africa is a passion that brings me to the African continent again and again. I had the privilege to live with five tribes and question everything I know about ethics, morality, mortality, womanhood, life, and birth. I've witnessed traditions and customs I could not fathom or understand.

I developed the ability to be a silent observer with the utmost respect and without questioning and imposing my belief system of what's right and wrong. Understanding that right and wrong are subjective and a product of cultural context is the biggest gift of my world travels and cultural encounters.

I remember going into a state of conflict at one of the tribal campsites. I was lost in my own shadow in the river, and I was thinking about what the hell was happening around me and how to even make sense of the ceremony. The western part of the world that I inhabit labels and categorizes everything, so making sense of the ceremony and practices that were being performed was not just challenging but hard to digest. I had a moment where I went from this confused and conflicted state of mind to the one of a silent observer. I changed my neuro chemistry within a few seconds, which was one of the self-help tools that I'd been developing. I had to mute and disregard the Sapna that loves to question and debate, the voice of feminists who just wants to champion women's rights and liberalism, and the stubborn Sapna who just has fire in her heart and who doesn't give up easily.

Once I muted that voice, I decided I would be an observer. I think that's when I found myself seeing life as is, and that is something I had never experienced before. Understanding that we are all living through one consciousness regardless of caste, creed, religion, or colour makes you experience gratitude, joy, and inner peace. After living with the tribes, I realised my truth is not the only truth. It's very uncomfortable to come across an entirely different truth. I had a realisation that observers don't question, they just stand with humility. That was one soul experience there.

After coming back to the United States from my African adventures, I competed in pageantry and became Miss Pakistan World 2021. This allowed me to materialize my lifelong dream of bringing martial arts education to vulnerable communities of the world. My karate academy is underway in Pakistan and Kenya. I know it's a very big tool that can change their lives and suddenly give them self-confidence. I have some tricks and tactics in my mind that I want to teach the girls if they ever find themselves in a challenging situation.

My three tips for an aspiring solo female traveller:

1. Learn to be street-smart and self-sufficient. Being street-smart has nothing to do with how well you can score on a test. One can become street-smart by learning the skills of negotiation, sound decision-making, self-reliance, and effective evaluations. These skills go a long way in navigating streets, getting along with people, and ultimately staying safe.

2. Always, always trust your gut and intuition. If something doesn't feel right and clenches your stomach, it probably isn't. Traveling alone strengthens our survival mechanism and sharpens our third eye. The more one travels and becomes comfortable with the discomforts that travelling brings, the more our intuition sharpens, thus allowing us to develop a sound understanding of the relationship and trust dynamics, uncertain territories, and our limits. I always let my intuition be my compass and guide and it has saved my life.

3. Create a community and meet other women travellers. Foster friendships and build ties and cultural bridges wherever you go. Meeting other women travellers and sharing and learning from their experiences gives us an irreplaceable gift of community that is pivotal in living a life of belonging, identity, and service. A close-knit community of fellow female travellers will allow us to inspire one another, be a listening ear, provide service, as well as help aspiring solo women travellers embark on their life-changing journeys.

Sapna is an athlete and engineer turned world traveller and entrepreneur who is growing a community of female martial artists and bringing travel stories of inspiring women, culture, and human grit.

Website: www.sapnasuitcase.com
Instagram: @sapnas_suitcase
YouTube: @sapnassuitcase7422

CONNECTING WITH NATURE

Livon Yeow

My very first relationship was with a South African man. I flew over to South Africa with him when I was 19 and during the six years we were together, we both went there every opportunity we got. Even after the relationship ended, I knew I wanted to go back to South Africa; it felt like home the very moment I stepped off the plane that first time. I've always loved wildlife and during my very first trip, I went to Kruger National Park, which is huge and spans three countries. I did my first safari and I fell in love with it.

Inspired by that trip, I booked a conservation project in the Eastern Cape, on the east coast of South Africa. I came across the project in a Conservation Volunteering Projects book that I received for Christmas from my brother. During the two-week project, I was out in the bush and surrounded by animals and other like-minded people from all over the world.

I made a lot of interesting new friends from all walks of life and ages. A few of them also wanted to do their Level 1 FGASA, a field/safari guide course, which piqued my curiosity. I had a full-time job at the time and didn't know when and how I would be able to do something like this. I returned to London life, but my curiosity was always there.

Six years later, I was running my life coaching and personal training business and thought, *This is the perfect time to go* — or as perfect as it was ever going to get. In 2019, I arrived in South Africa for two months to do my Level 1 FGASA training. This started a whole new adventure for me. It changed things in the sense that I knew that if I wanted to spend more time out in the bush, then having an online business wouldn't work anymore, or at least not full-time. The key reason is that there isn't Wi-Fi in the bush, which makes client contact impossible. I went back into full-time employment to build something for the future in a more sustainable way.

One of the earliest defining moments of this particular trip was in Mashatu, Botswana for the first month of the course. It was the first night in camp and we were sleeping on the floor of our tents. There was a herd of elephants in the camp that night. Imagine lying on the floor and you've got three to six-tonne elephants around you and their shadows moving across your tent. You can hear them chewing, dropping dung, and their stomachs rumbling right above you. It was terrifying.

I felt very small at that moment, even though I know they won't intentionally kill me, my thinking was that they could bring down a tree that squashes the tent, or accidentally step on the tent itself. Life could have been over just like that. I think the fascinating thing for me was that it never happened despite the many elephants that came through most nights and broke the water tank (in the dry season) more than once. That was magical.

I had more than one moment of thinking that this was how we used to live, and how far removed we are from that primitive way of life today. But this is how things should be. I felt a sense of connectedness with all living things. It was one of those defining moments; the fact that they knew we were there, we knew they were there, and there was no fear. Eventually, at the end of that first month, I got used to it. I realised that all humans fear things they don't understand and aren't exposed to.

Another one of those moments was when we spotted a lioness out on a drive. She was nursing and had taken a break from new mother duties. After a short lie-down, she got up, looked right at us and led us back to her den. In the wild, newborn cubs aren't even introduced to the rest of the pride until around two months of age. As she approached, four cubs ran out to greet her; they were tiny! It was as if she wanted to show off her cubs. It was just such a special moment because we knew that this wasn't normal and it showed the level of trust between wildlife and humans, where trust has developed in this area over time.

I was nervous about going into the bush in a group environment and being stuck with the same people with no way out if I didn't like them for two whole months. The majority of the group ended up being much younger than me and it brought up memories of being at school where I felt like the odd one out, not quite fitting in (and also not particularly wanting to). The group played volleyball a lot too and team sports was something I had never really been good at or participated in much.

I ended up tackling that fear by finding areas of commonality; with the younger girls, we were the minority in the group, and with others who were slightly older, or had a similar reference point to me, who could understand the same humour. This helped me to break down the fear, make a few friends, be more present, and enjoy the experience a little more.

The other fear I had was budgeting correctly, especially with unexpected costs. In Malawi, I didn't know anyone, and I ended up needing to find the cash to cover accommodation. In the end, I got creative, and having recently completed my Level 2 Reiki initiation, offered reiki sessions online and in-person for as little as £10, which helped me cover costs.

While money is important, it is not my primary motivation, it's not the thing that excites me. It's being out in nature and being switched off from technology for big chunks of time. I realised how peaceful, content, and present I am when I'm in the bush, and nothing else compares. It's like a state of constant flow. I'm not thinking about the future or the past, I'm always in the present. That's what sparked everything; I hadn't experience that anywhere else — being connected to the environment and the world.

I'm a big believer in facing your fears and trying new things, which is why I chose to do white-water rafting in Zambia. It's one of the top things to do in Livingstone, and people come from all over the world to do the Zambezi river and experience level 5 rapids. I'm not a water person or a good swimmer. I was terrified of being in the water even though I had a life jacket. Each rapid had a name and the commentator would tell us that we're now approaching 'Terminator 1' 'Terminator 2,' and 'Stairway to Heaven.' Suddenly, our boat flipped and half of us went overboard. I was terrified as the force of the water pushed me under. I didn't know which way was up and felt like I was just swallowing gallons of water. It was probably only a minute or so but felt like an eternity! It felt like a life-or-death situation and probably something I wouldn't do again.

My travels to Africa made me 'grow up' in the traditional sense of the word. I'd never really been interested in savings, mortgages, or investments before. I was tapping into a passion, something that I enjoyed and wanted to spend more time doing, which inspired me to finally start to put plans in place and think more long-term in terms of my life and what I wanted it to look like.

My three tips for an aspiring solo female traveller:

1. Talk to the people of the country as soon as you get on the ground. Try to connect with them as soon as you land.
2. Do things as locals would do as much as possible. Walk, ride a bike, and ask for food spot recommendations that locals would go to.
3. Create your support system in advance and within the country itself if possible. Ask people in your network about who they know in the country you're going to, make connections on the ground ahead of time, and get local tips and advice. It's about being resourceful.

Liv Yeow is the founder of LivLife BIGGER®, an organisation focused on empowering, inspiring, and connecting individuals and organisations for positive change. She has delivered talks (inc. a TEDx in 2019) and workshops around Fear, Freedom, Resilience, and work-life alignment through it. Liv is a Life Coach with a diverse clientele, ranging from teachers and creatives to Fintech professionals, helping them to transform their lives and wellbeing. She also has a Market Research and Strategy background, has worked as a Personal Trainer and Reiki Practitioner, and is a qualified FGASA Field/Safari Guide.

Vaishali Patel

Liv has travelled extensively - solo backpacking from 19 years old to over 40 countries, and currently calls both the UK and South Africa home. In 2021, she started training to be a Trails Guide and in between planning backpack trails, safari retreats, and studying wine (more recently), she is also writing a book of lessons from the bush.

Website: www.livlifebigger.com
Instagram: @livlifebigger

FOLLOWING MY INSPIRATION

Victoria von Stein

I'm a creative designer with a French and German background. Growing up in different countries offered me an open mind and a love for travel, cultures, and languages. As my friends got married and had children, it got more difficult to plan holidays abroad together. I wasn't on that same path in my early 30s, so I started to reflect on other paths I wanted to create for myself that felt fulfilling and exciting. I decided that I wanted to explore, discover, and experience adventures that would enrich my creativity and my own life. My challenge was to overcome my fear of travelling solo as a woman to achieve my dreams.

After plenty of research and introspective moments, I wanted my travel experiences to have a purpose. Developing my creativity and artistic skills made travelling more meaningful to me. To my delight, I found a creative travel company (FRUI HOLIDAYS) where I could learn new travel photography skills and have Kerala in India as my canvas while travelling safely with a small group of people. This inspired me to go for it.

There were not many blogs written about solo female travel and I felt blessed that my mother encouraged me to go for it because she knew how much I wanted it. You have to be surrounded by people who help you and support you in your goals and dreams. Stay away from naysayers, as they advise according to their ideas, which doesn't help you. I felt confident once I bought the ticket and talked to the friendly tour company. Buying the ticket made me overcome the fear of the unknown, as I had invested in the trip now and I had to do it. By just taking the action, you move forward instead of trying to figure it out in your head. It felt thrilling and exciting!

One morning, we woke up at 4am and drove up to the highest mountain to photograph the sunrise. The journey up the mountain was not safe at all. It was rocky and we were in a very old jeep and on one side, you could fall, so you had to hold on tight. I experienced this beautiful wonder of nature with fellow travellers I'd just met. That was a proud moment for me as I dared to go for it, to follow what inspired me. After that, anything is possible.

The journey taught me to trust myself as well as my inner guidance and intuition. I learnt that it's ok to go for what you want in your life, and you're allowed to follow your desires and dreams. You must dare to follow your inspirations. It opened me up to connect with strangers and communicate with wonderful people in Kerala. I learnt I could get along with anyone if there was tolerance, understanding, and respect. I love the thrill of discovering new cultures, so it wasn't that difficult for me to be present in the moment, soak in all the beautiful surroundings, architecture, smells, colours, and a new language. I wanted to milk the experiences when I came back and do something meaningful with it, so I created a jewellery collection from it.

At first, it was more like a hobby that I did alongside my job as a graphic designer. I took classes in learning how to create jewellery with silver and traditional craftsmanship. Inspired by my travel to Kerala, I decided to evoke my adventurous memories through jewellery as these precious objects are worn on the body, next to your heart. I infused scenes of warm sunlight on the skin, colourful houses, radiant palm trees, and the famous backwaters and rolling hills into my designs.

The trip gave me a direction for my jewellery, it gave me a purpose for why I make jewellery. I learned a lot about myself, about being brave and what lights me up.

I wanted to create jewellery that empowers women to go for their dreams, go for what they want and take inspired action for what they want to create in their life. It started with this trip because I did it for myself. I overcame fears of travelling alone, and I discovered a new country, which gave me new energy when I came back. I needed to nourish my soul, my creativity, and my curiosity to help breathe new life, and new originality into my work.

I highly recommend joining a small group at the beginning, to just ease yourself into the feeling of what it would be like to travel on your own but still be in a safe container, so the travel company takes care of everything. You don't have to worry about hotels and transport, all you have to organise and schedule is your flights, your luggage, and what you need to bring. For me, it was okay because it was like a soft launch into travelling on my own but within a safe container. That gave me a springboard to then go one step further and go completely on my own.

My next enriching and meaningful trip was to Bali. This was a solo travel journey where I went without a supporting group. I was worried about what would happen if I got sick or if I had an accident and was trying to figure it out in my head. It created unnecessary worry again. What helped me to overcome my worry about the unknown was booking the flight and arriving at the destination. Every time I got to my end destination, the worries just went away. I remember telling myself that everything was going to be okay and I'm never alone. Again, I had the most wonderful experience of my life.

After travel photography, I decided that I would like to try the local craftsmanship skills of each country I went to. I thought it would be a good way to learn more about their culture and that it would give me more of a connection with the locals. In Bali, I did a local craft course class in Batik design. I met this wonderful master who taught me his ancient, family craft traditions. I felt so nourished having learnt new skills and how to work with wood and bamboo. I made a little bamboo dragonfly, which I gave to a little boy on the streets. It's these little moments of joy and meaningful connections with local people that I constantly remember. In Thailand, I did a ceramics class and a Thai cooking class. I always do workshops as I find them the best way to experience the culture. As a result, I learn more about what I'm interested in.

Bali was my most enriching solo travel experience spiritually. I enjoyed meeting new people through the craft workshops I enrolled in. It was a self-led, self-initiated, self-directed journey to discover this beautiful Hindu culture. It inspired me to create illustrations that help us find ways of connecting to the art of living in a harmonious, balanced way with nature, our surroundings and our inner soul.

My three tips for an aspiring solo female traveller:

1. Ask yourself, what makes you want to go travelling on your own, what gives you purpose, and what would make it a meaningful experience? Then follow that desire, that joy, that initial inspired action that makes you want to go.
2. Book your flight. Don't think too much, just book your flight and figure out the details later. Once you put financial investment in it, you're already invested, it's scheduled, and you're going to do it.
3. Trust your inner guidance and your intuition. Travel has helped me develop a closer relationship with my soul, my inner guidance, and hearing that voice that guides me.

Victoria von Stein, is a graphic and jewellery designer artist based in London. Her solo travel experiences inspired her handcrafted fine jewellery and illustrations.

Website: www.victoriavonstein.com

BEING BOLDER

Annabel Harper MA, FRSA

My future of doing the Inca Trail was questioned when I discovered I had a brain tumour. It was benign but I had become quite unwell, and I was disappointed because it was something that I was looking forward to doing. It was a charity trek organised by the British Heart Foundation to Machu Picchu.

It took me about six months to recuperate and then I went back to work at the BBC as a journalist. Out of the blue, I got another flyer about going to Peru and I thought maybe this was my opportunity for me to give back. I felt thankful that my surgery was successful. Because, even if you have a benign brain tumour, sometimes, they're not operable, and I was very lucky. I spoke to my GP about my plans to go and he told me to go for it after getting checked out and doing a medical. The original intention had been to go on my own and after sharing with some friends of mine, a friend said she'd like to join. I was feeling excited and a bit nervous. I sought sponsorship and did lots of preparation and walking.

It was exciting to be in South America for the first time. We landed, and before we knew it, off we went and set off on our trek to Machu Picchu. We had porters who took small bags for us to where we were going to stay and therefore had to pack very lightly. Each night, it got colder and colder, but it was beautiful. I did have altitude sickness which was quite a struggle. There were times when it was hard work, but the beautiful scenery made it worthwhile. It was worth every step because when we did finally get to Machu Picchu, it was just extraordinary.

I walked on my own quite a bit during the trek and had lots of time for reflection. It was the first time that I had to really examine my story and how I got there. There was something different about this choice that I made. The trek gave me a sense of agency and confidence that I didn't have before. I was in control of myself and my life, and I could do more than I thought I could.

I was worried that I wouldn't be able to manage it physically. Although I was pretty fit, I didn't know what impact altitude sickness would have, and I discovered that you might feel it at one altitude and not another. I got to the highest point and was fine when lots of people were unwell. The next day, I felt it. People had gone to Kilimanjaro, for instance, and they didn't experience altitude sickness whereas they did at Machu Picchu.

I felt a sense of achievement because I'd been able to do it and a couple of people couldn't. It was very hard, and I just focused on each step and each day. We had great cheerleaders in the guides that we had and the people from the British Heart Foundation who had done this before. People had helped me when I was struggling and there was a real collaborative spirit. A few people would gather around and walk with anyone lagging, so nobody was left behind. We were in it together.

Someone that inspired me on the trek was an older lady who had recently been widowed. She came to give back to the British Heart Foundation because her husband had heart problems. She'd never done anything on her own, so it was a big deal for her, and she just kept going. She was experiencing a lot of sadness as she'd been married for years, and her family was telling her that she was crazy to do this at her age. She was determined to finish and didn't feel sorry for herself. She didn't give up.

The whole experience was new for me, and I just enjoyed every bit of it. I'd never seen landscapes like that before. I'd never been in that kind of culture before, and I'd never been to South America either. I found it stimulating to see the colourful national dresses. Lots of people still wear it. There's a lot of history and I felt it very present while we were walking. It was quite extraordinary to me that Machu Picchu was only re-discovered in the early

1900s even though it's believed to have been built in the 15th century. The people were quite clever with how they built structures and how people worked all this stuff out, without all the equipment that we have now.

I've always enjoyed travelling and I love new things. I don't play safe so much. That might be partly because I'm older and I'm more comfortable in my skin and I think that's quite important to us. My trip to Peru was enabling, in that sense. It was one of the hardest things I've ever done, and it was truly rewarding. One thing that I look back on and smile at is dancing like mad and laughing hard after we finished the trek at the hotel. We were so euphoric to have finished!

The trip was emotional for me. I realised that I had not appreciated that I could do much more than I thought I could because, physically, it was very difficult. It made me begin to think about what I wanted in life. Having gone through the experience of a brain tumour gave me a different perspective. I was prepared to try things that I probably may not consider trying before. I was being bolder.

I began to wonder if there was more that I could do in my career than what I was doing. I had moved into a management role by then at the BBC and I worked with a huge team of journalists and loved being involved with the newsroom. I had fantastic experiences as a journalist.

From the day I left university, I was always interested in people, and I got involved in people development work when I was in this role. I enjoyed that, and coaching came up as a suggestion from somebody who at the time was my mentor. I did lots of research and it excited me, and I don't believe in regrets; I think they are a waste of energy. I thought, if I don't do this, I might regret it. That led me to leave the BBC and go back to university to do a master's in coaching. I was very fortunate to find work at a business school, which was wonderful and helped me to build up my own business.

It was at the beginning of the recession in 2008 when an opportunity came up to go to the Middle East, which I never would have considered. But having done Machu Picchu, I developed the attitude to step into things much more. I took the opportunity and worked in the Middle East, which then led me to do a master's in Middle Eastern studies, followed by writing my book, *Shujaa'ah: Bold Leadership for Women of the Middle East*. I'm not sure how much of that would have been done without going to Machu Picchu; I think that was a turning point for me.

My three tips for an aspiring solo female traveller:

1. Make sure you've got a clean pair of socks if you're walking every day. It doesn't matter about the rest — clean socks every day. Look after your feet.
2. Make sure that you've got plenty of loo roll and antiseptic wipes.
3. Always drink bottled water. Never drink tap water, even when cleaning your teeth.

Annabel is an author, speaker, and executive coach. Her book, "Shujaa'ah: Bold Leadership for Women of the Middle East" explores the vibrant culture in the region. Ever the traveller, Annabel is energised and drawn towards new horizons of all kinds.

Website: www.changeconnections.com
Linkedin: annabelharper

IT'S ALL POSSIBLE

Flo Sabeva

I was living a very comfortable life in Belgium. I was teaching full-time and doing a bit of music but not being as creative as I would have liked. I was holding back my creativity. I was not living the life I wanted to have. My engagement had broken off when I realised he wasn't the right person for me, and I needed a new start.

I chose to leave Belgium, selling all my furniture and putting other things in storage, and go to Boston. I chose to go to Boston, USA to study at one of the largest schools in music, the Berkley College of Music. I thought that it would be a good opportunity for me because I studied classical music before and this college focused on pop music compositions, where there is more freedom to create songs.

When I got there, things didn't turn out exactly how I imagined. I realised that the school was not a big school of music, and I didn't enjoy being there. I stayed six months in Boston before I ran out of money because I was paying for everything myself. I didn't have any money coming from anywhere, and I didn't have any support, so I had to stop attending school. I decided to put all my money into the trip and that I would find a way to make more money when I got to the US, but I didn't. I had to come back to Europe in the end because I ran out of money. From this experience, I learnt that I must manage my money better when I go on trips.

Before going back to Belgium, I decided to take a 10-day trip from LA to San Francisco because this was something I always dreamed of. I ended up meeting the sister of one of my flatmates and we discovered the city together. It was one of the most memorable experiences of my life. The trip changed something inside of me. It enabled me to be with myself.

Renting a car and going on a road trip from LA to San Francisco was something I had never done before. I organised exactly where I wanted to go before doing the trip so I could enjoy the freedom of being on the journey there. Driving along the ocean, listening to Norah Jones, meeting nice people, and having a sense of freedom, I'll never forget that feeling. I enjoyed every moment of taking in the ocean view and I felt it in every cell of my body. I was feeling happy.

I grew a lot through introspection. I was meditating and read a lot of books. I read the book, *Eat, Pray, Love* by Elizabeth Gilbert, and it helped me make peace with myself and be happier within. I was feeling more confident about my creativity and learning to follow my intuition and trust myself.

It was a good way to learn about who I was being away from family and conferences. I was asking questions such as: Who am I? What do I like to do? What do I want to do? Being on my own opened me up and made me accessible to myself and others. I was shy and an introvert and would never go to a party on my own or speak to people that I didn't know. I didn't want to be alone, so I went up to people and spoke to them. I saw people just have a conversation for five minutes in Starbucks and then go. This was different from Belgium where people don't talk to you for five minutes and go. I experienced a change in myself where I wasn't afraid to talk to strangers anymore.

I met a new person in San Diego, and we had a coffee together. I remember feeling so at peace with myself. Being heard and having a chat with her was nice; she became a good friend, whom I'm still in touch with.

I didn't want to go back to Europe. I felt disappointed on a professional level, but I was coming back a changed person. I entered a new part of my life, where I decided I want to be creative, write music, and be a composer. It wasn't easy for the first five years to produce music, but I just did it and once I started doing it, I couldn't stop. When I finished studying, I had to choose classical music or another category; you couldn't do more than one together. It was refreshing that I could still be a classical musician and create and write music at the same time. It's all possible.

My three tips for an aspiring solo female traveller:

1. Organise by researching the things you want to do but then, on the trip, be flexible because sometimes you expect to see or do something, and it doesn't turn out that way. Sometimes, you find a spot that was not in your plan or you didn't schedule, but it is amazing, and you need to stop and just enjoy the moment.
2. Get good insurance. Think about your safety.
3. Budget for the trip and keep a little extra for any surprises.

TAKING CONTROL OF MY LIFE

Lynn Wisniewski

I attended a silent Vipassana meditation retreat where you don't speak for ten days. The retreat was four hours away from my home in Florida, which isn't far, but it was an emotional time for me and a much-needed adventure. I had just gone through a divorce and had recently given birth to my son.

While getting hair therapy one day, my hairdresser was talking about a silent meditation retreat. I wasn't very familiar with meditation at the time, but I knew I had to go. I signed up for the retreat but couldn't go until six months later when an opening became available, and everything just fell into place. I had my son, and it was the first time I was going to leave him for a few days. It was hard to give up time with him and do something for me, yet I knew this was something that I was called to do.

I cried for most of the car journey to the retreat. I was scared and nervous and then once I got past a certain point, I kept talking to myself saying, "If I'm going to do this, I can't sit and cry." At that moment, I decided I was going to give it my all. When I arrived at my destination, I wrote a little love note and put it with a rose in my car so when I completed the retreat and came back to my car, I would surprise myself and feel special.

The retreat was so beautiful. Peace, quiet, no agenda, nowhere I had to be or anyone I had to deal with or anything to figure out. I just got to be and be with myself. I was with other people in the space, but we couldn't look at each other or talk to one another and I did it to the tee. It was wonderful and, in the end, we were encouraged to talk with one another so we could get back into society. Many of the other attendees thought I was foreign, which was interesting to hear people's take on me based on what they saw visually.

It was a huge thing for me to do for the first time on my own. I didn't have to think about anybody else or worry about the day-to-day parts of life; I had to be fully present. When I came home, everybody was curious about how I would have changed. I noticed I was not reacting to things like I had been before and that was a refreshing change.

Travelling before this I had always relied on a parent to take on the responsibilities. When travelling to the UK with my son to visit a friend for the first time, I found it quite a different experience. I didn't have a responsible person to tell me what to do. I remember we went to get food at the airport, and they were calling our names on the loudspeaker to board our flight! At that point, I realised that I had to pay attention, I had to be the responsible person, and I had to look out for myself, as well as my son. Before this, I found myself resisting responsibility and now I realize it made me more confident in who I am. We have such wonderful memories from our trip abroad together and not only did my young son gain a lot, but so did I!

Travelling solo had a huge impact on me and my confidence increased every time I did it. I remember I booked tickets to see Jason Mraz in concert in a small town in Western New York and I drove up by myself. I got in my car in Florida at 8pm and drove all the way and it was so peaceful. I had an open window and was singing my heart out the whole drive up. It was wonderful. I slept for two hours at the rest stop when the sun came up. I felt that was safer than in the dark. It's good to think smart and safe, and not be afraid to just go and do it. I saw deer on either side of the road, and I was terrified that one was going to run in front of my car. I told myself that I can worry about this, or I can handle it if it happens, and it might not ever happen. I made it just in time for the concert, all deer in tack.

While driving, my pressure gauge came on in my car saying my tire pressure was low. I stopped the car, and when I looked at my tires, there was a piece of metal stuck in one of them. I was calm and used my phone to find the nearest garage. When I got there, they couldn't fix it, but they were helpful by sending me to somebody else who was open to helping. The thing about solo travel is that you are never alone, as there are people out there who genuinely look out for you. I don't think people are out to get me. I heard many people say to be careful or go with someone, and I've been fortunate in all my travels alone to have kind souls along the way.

I gave the guy that fixed my tire $40 and half the peaches I picked up when I got to North Carolina. It was nice being around these little old men talking about politics and being grumpy in the waiting room of the garage. It was good to be kind and aware of my surroundings and situations.

The casual drive home coasting through back roads over 22 hours was so calming. I chose the back roads instead of the fast highways coming back to Florida from New York and I enjoyed every minute of it.

This road trip helped me to see my greatness and that we are all capable of being and doing anything! I have more appreciation for who I am and what I've accomplished; it empowered me and helped me to take it easier on myself. I've been able to look inward and say, "Good job," and take time to stop, enjoy, and appreciate what I have done and the people in my life. I don't have to keep striving every day to do more.

When I came home, so many people were surprised that I did this road trip by myself. I realised that it sounds so much scarier when you think about doing something and over analyse what could happen. When you just get out and do it, the adventure is so much fun!!

From my solo trips, I continue to learn that I can do anything. Travelling on my own and not analysing or letting fear or worry take over has been life changing. I created a gift shop right after I did the silent retreat, which is filled with art by local artists and a lot of love. The retreat got me to be more centred, more in the moment and to really be with people, instead of in my brain. Asking for help when I needed it and how willing people are to help is amazing. I think that being alone and driving felt like I was taking control of my life. I realised responsibility is not a bad thing and taking charge of my life can be very empowering.

My three tips for an aspiring solo female traveller:

1. Be prepared, but don't overthink things.
2. Just do it.
3. Trust that you will be taken care of. If you feel a desire, you are capable of fulfilling that desire. It is life's way of telling you, "Hey, come on let's do this!"

Writer, artist, entrepreneur, and coach, Lynn Wisniewski, is an avid traveller who loves exploring the world and all the beauty it offers while inspiring others to do the same.

Website: www.growyoursoul.love

TRUST THE PROCESS

Dr Nikki Izadi

I had told myself I would take a gap year or sabbatical ever since I left school. Despite many short trips, 15 years had passed, and I had not taken the dedicated time to travel that I had once promised myself. The thought of travelling solo both excited and terrified me. I was plagued with guilty thoughts like, *What if it's not safe to travel alone as a woman? Will my family be ok? I have a great job. What if I don't find something else as good? I should really focus on settling down and meeting someone.* I worked my way through some of these concerns and found solutions to most things, but what continued to hold me back was my job.

I was 33 years old and worked as a dentist in a practice that was a 10-minute walk from my flat where, over the years, I had built a list of patients whom I had grown fond of. It didn't feel like the right time to quit my job, especially without anything else in place, but then, would it ever be? Deep down, I knew I wanted to fulfil the promise I made to my younger self many years before, and if not now, then when? Eventually, it took a dear friend's wedding in Brunei to encourage me to bite the bullet. I bought a one-way ticket.

I attended my best friend's wedding and began the next leg of my adventure with a two-week diving trip to the Philippines. I had no idea where I was going to go next. It excited me to follow my instincts and not make too many plans; to be as free as a bird in a big wide world. I knew that I wanted to split my trip into two parts. The first would be for me to explore, learn about different cultures and meet new people, as well as to nurture

70

myself by reading, writing, eating well, meditating, and partaking in adventure. The latter part of the trip would be about giving back to the world, somehow. I wanted more purpose and meaning in my life, and although I was grateful for the work that I did day-to-day, I wanted to create something outside of dentistry.

I had been very cautious so far in my adulthood years. The whole process of travelling felt daunting, from dreaming about it to the execution. Yet, I challenged myself to face my fears and go beyond my comfort zone. That was the main driving force for me; I knew I wanted more from life and had some growing to do. I felt that this could be the perfect time to apply some of the personal learning I had accumulated over the years. I had recently exited a long-term relationship with a great man which didn't work out. I was determined to come back renewed and ready to start a new chapter, aligned with the woman that I wanted to be for myself and those around me.

The first leg of the trip was full of adventure, from receiving my PADI certificate after which, I dived off the shores of Palawan Island witnessing an array of colourful reef fish, to visiting ancient temples in the Angkor Thom complex. I learned about the healing properties of plants in the rainforests of Malaysia, attended soul-enriching yoga retreats, and stayed in straw huts in sleepy villages. I also witnessed evidence of human beings at their worst, in the brutally cruel S-21 interrogation centres of Cambodia. It truly was the 'eat, pray, love' experience I'd wished for mixed with a wake-up call of the suffering of mankind. The more people I met and places I went to, the richer the experience and the more I felt at home.

By this point, three months had passed, and it was time for the second leg of the trip. Before travelling, I had participated in an advanced year-long growth and development course called Wisdom, which focussed on upgrading those cyclical conversations we engage in as adults and bringing play to life. I distinctly remember a light bulb moment on the program, and I knew it was the start of something being born, something I was being called into. As I was sitting in my seat intently listening to the program leader speak, I heard her say something fascinating: "We are speaking beings and our tool is language. Our experience of life exists through our network of conversations. If you want to transform something, transform the network of conversations." It sounded simple, yet it felt profound. It made me reflect on the conversations that kept coming up around the Middle East, and my heritage.

I am half Iranian from my paternal side, and I lived in Iran until I was six years old. During this defining part of my childhood, the Iran-Iraq war took place. As a little girl, I hated what I saw of the war. I remember seeing worn-out faces, the fear in my mother's eyes every time my father would leave Tehran for work, going into the basement shelter during air raids, and images of men in crutches with blown-off limbs. I remember a deep desire to help people as a child.

As I grew older and learnt of other conflicts in the world, especially in the Middle East, it stirred something unresolved in my soul. I had attended a few talks and protests about the Israeli-Palestinian conflict, and I was blown away by the dedication of people who devoted their lives to the mission of peace.

What had opened for me on the Wisdom program, was this: history kept repeating itself. What hadn't changed was the narrative, the network of conversations. That was the moment an idea came: What if I could contribute something back to this domain? It was so far from anything I knew or deeply studied. And at the same time, I believe that, alongside the government and framework of the society we live in, we each also have individual responsibility for what happens in the world, and the worst thing we can do is to sit back and do nothing. I didn't for a moment think I could change the world, but what I did think was this: I could do something. Whilst I contemplated the words of the Wisdom program leader, I thought about the Middle East peace situation, which was an area close to my heart. Perhaps the only way things in the Middle East were ever going to change was to generate a new network of conversations and somehow 'interrupt' the same narrative about this region.

I had the start of a vision about what it was I wanted to do on the second part of my trip. I wanted to travel to one part of the Middle East and start a small personal project: to meet change-makers from the ground and share their stories with a view of discovering the region newly from the perspective of activists or those dedicated to a cause in their field of interest and who were making a difference to their wider community. Perhaps if I was able to put aside my personal views, including giving up my resignation about what's possible in the region, learn newly, and transform my narrative of the Middle East, then others could do the same too.

The Middle East and its complex history fascinated me. I wanted to feed my mind and the mind of others with a side to the Middle East we don't usually think of or talk about, the inspiring side. It felt surreal that I was about to embark on something so far removed from my day job. I chose Lebanon to travel to. It was somewhere I'd never been before, a small enough country to navigate and yet geographically and strategically of importance. It was on the border with Israel and Syria, with a huge number of refugees from either end; it had been through war with Israel, civil war, and had a fractioned society of multiple cultures, religions, and political views, all living side by side.

When I initially told my family, I had mixed responses. My dad was supportive. He always taught me to be courageous, and he liked the idea and could sympathise with the reason why I wanted to do this. My mum was anxious and worried for my safety. She asked me, "What if you disappear? What if you don't come back? What if you're doing something just because you're being idealistic and end up being kidnapped?" Although I took on board the concerns of my friends and family, it did not stop me. I had this inner belief that I was going to be okay, although I'm not sure where that came from. I thought to myself, *If I am careful and have my wits about me, I will be fine.* I planned on sharing my whereabouts each day with at least one member of my family.

Another reason I chose Lebanon was because, at the time I was planning the trip, I was being supported by two friends: Nai, who is originally Lebanese, and her then fiancé, Chace. We created weekly calls leading up to the time I travelled, and they were to meet me in Lebanon towards the end of my time there. When I arrived, Nai put me in touch with her father, Nassif, who picked me up from the airport. He was an ex-military guy from the Lebanese army. He helped me find an Airbnb as he knew the owner, which made me feel safe from the start.

On the journey from the airport to my accommodation, Nassif asked me about the purpose of my trip and how he could help. I started sharing a little bit about why I came. He listened intently and told me he wanted to introduce me to a friend of his. I was excited and surprised that it was only the beginning and already I was meeting people to talk about my project. They asked me many questions and paid scrupulous attention to my response. I left that meeting feeling somewhat disheartened and found myself wondering whether I was being foolish and I started to doubt myself.

At the same time, I knew that I had responded to Nassif and his friend in a typically British, self-deprecating, and apologetic manner. I had quickly learnt, within the first few days of being there, that Lebanon was full of sophisticated and highly educated people, who were understandably cynical about the West. I knew I had to adjust my tone and communicate in a way that was acceptable and convincing.

I met Marie, who had worked for five different NGOs in senior positions, and I shared my project idea with her. She told me she found it refreshing and she offered to help me with the project and introduce me to others too. It was a very organic process after that.

I was planning to collect stories of inspiring people and share their stories in written form. That changed when I met a fellow traveller with a passion for photography at the Airbnb I was staying in. He asked if I had considered making videos instead of writing. He suggested the kind of stories that I wanted to share were probably very emotive, and I could capture much more on video. I agreed with him, although I was camera shy and did not have the adequate skills or equipment to take quality videos. I realised these were my barriers, and that there were people with those skill sets who could help me. My job was to find those people and inspire them in the vision of the project. It did happen, in some magical way. I somehow met the right people at the right time, all of whom became involved voluntarily.

I was now with a team of people, I had a filmmaker on board, and we had borrowed high-end camera equipment and voice recorders, all free of charge. Everyone who got involved had a similar vision and wanted to change the narrative of the Middle East. They wanted to be known and understood and for people from the West to witness the real human beings that existed in the heart of Lebanese society. We interviewed 18 inspiring people.

The experience in Lebanon made me step out and get involved in a way that I never thought I would. My role as an impromptu journalist and how I engaged with each person was key to how well they came across in the videos. The more relaxed and connected I was with them, the more the process flowed, and their humanity shone through. I created a 'connecting' exercise with each person, which we performed before starting the interview. This involved sitting or standing nearby opposite each other in silence and 'being with' each other for approximately a minute. This allowed us to relax into the space between each other and start to discover who each other was, in the shortest amount of time through the eyes. Those were pockets of time that seemed to stand still, and whereby momentarily, I was able to step into the world of a stranger. I have a very funny story that I often share with friends, about one of the guys whom I interviewed who tried to kiss me after one of these exercises, and the absolute shock of that! Generally, however, in most instances, it served its purpose.

I feel that the account of my time in Lebanon would not be complete without sharing some examples of the interviews, which added a much deeper and richer layer to my travelling experience. Everyone had a whole world to share, and I would have loved to have followed them further with their stories and taken background footage to showcase their work. However, time was indeed the limiting factor.

Mohammad Ayoub is the founder of an organisation called NAHNOO. His organisation is a youth-led NGO rallying volunteers across Lebanon to work towards an inclusive society through various campaigns. He started this as a student at university and many years later, it's still going strong. The NGO has directly affected change in the law, based on their timely and relevant advocacy campaigns that promote good governance, public spaces, and the protection of cultural heritage. One project that I was inspired by when interviewing Mohammad related to a public space which was closed to the public in 1995 by the Municipality of Beirut and was only open to Western foreigners. In 2010, Nahnoo organised a 'Reopen Horsh Beirut' campaign, alongside other NGOs. After five years of campaigning and awareness raising, the park opened to the public in 2015. It is now the largest park in the capital city, which has very few green spaces to enjoy, for all to use.

I met Rania Barghout, in an old Beirut theatre, which she bought to pursue a youth project close to her heart. Rania, a previous news presenter who once interviewed Hilary Clinton, is the founder of Rockstars Talent Management, where she trains young creatives to develop their stage skills in public speaking, dance, singing, and acting. She shared her personal story of her struggles being a successful, famous woman in Lebanese society and her desire to stay true to her purpose and to use her position to make a difference to upcoming talents.

Ziad Abi Chaker, who calls himself the 'King of Garbage,' is one of the most inspiring people I met. I recall walking into his office which is made completely of recyclable materials, from his desk to the flooring and the cabinetry. Lebanon used to have a huge rubbish problem, mostly due to the mishandling of waste. Ziad is an environmental engineer who has found many solutions to Lebanon's rubbish crisis. His company, Cedar Environmental, has revolutionised waste management, where the waste either becomes compost for farmers or other recycling initiatives such as glassware, fibres, furniture, and solid panels to replace steel and wood.

Another way I developed from my time in Lebanon was my love of good food. I wouldn't say I was a foodie before my trip to Lebanon, but I soon became one and Lebanese food still stands as my favourite cuisine. I went to a famous café in the heart of Beirut, one of the many Tawlets, which function like a farmer's kitchen, created by the founder, Kamal Mouzawak. During my interview with Kamal, he described his upbringing in rural Lebanon. His grandfather and uncle were farmers, and his family mainly ate produce from their garden. Many years later, his passion for gastronomy led him to become the founder of Souk El Tayeb, where he brought food from rural farmers' markets into the city. In doing so, he also had a mission to promote peace and unite Lebanese society: "If we live on the same land and we have the same agriculture, then we share the same cuisine. Food is something you share with the other, that includes the other, rather than excluding them." He feels that food unites people, "We can kill each other because of our differences, or we can find a common ground," reflected Kamal. In his mission, he also wanted to empower women from the fringes of Lebanese society who are passionate about cooking to come to the city and cook and serve in the cafes.

I'm still in touch with some of the people that I met in Lebanon. The filmmaker, Maysoon, shared with me later that she had transformed as a person after being involved in the project; it gave her hope and inspiration. She went on to continue filming similar stories after I left, and recently got a scholarship to study international relations. She told me, "Nikki, you came here to create a change and as simple as change looks, it doesn't happen before we change ourselves." Doing the project together, and meeting people from different backgrounds and sharing their stories, gave her a wider perspective. With the knowledge she gained, she realised she wanted to change lives, and so it was all destined in her studying international relations for her master's.

I discovered through my experience with the project in Lebanon that God's planning is way better than my own, and if I take actions outside my comfort zone into the unknown, synchronicities and magic happen. If I put myself in the unfamiliar, stand in my vision and trust the process, anything is possible. With this newfound attitude, on my return from my travels, I created the career of my dreams, working as a dentist in a private practice in London after previously working in the National Health Service.

Fast forward a few years, and I am currently transitioning into the next exciting stage of creating a new model for practising dentistry inside of setting up my own business, which will be centred around service and community focused. I believe I developed the courage and leap of faith to create and fulfil these lifelong dreams from my travelling experience.

One truth that I learnt first-hand from this experience, which I have carried with me day to day since, is this: Every human being wants to be known for who they are. It's up to us if we want to get to know the real human being or stick with the ideas in our heads and narratives about them.

My three tips for an aspiring solo female traveller:

1. Just do it. It's different to travelling with family or friends. You get to learn about yourself, and what gets you going, and it may change the course of your life. If it's something that inspires you, then just do it. It doesn't have to be a year-long trip, as long as you're stretching yourself and stepping outside your comfort zone.
2. Speak to strangers as much as possible, whilst being mindful of keeping safe. Don't hold back. It's so easy to feel awkward and withdraw when you're scared, but you get to discover who you are as a person when you are meeting new people and expanding your horizons.
3. Start with a community, and don't be afraid to use contacts. The very first place I went to on my own was a yoga retreat and being part of a group helped me feel safe. If you are scared like I was, that will make you feel a lot safer. Then you will naturally gain confidence and know what to do next. Trust the process.

I am a holistic dentist in London with a commitment to living life to the full and being a contribution. At the core of my being, what I really care about and stand for is peace on the planet.

Instagram: @dr.nikki.izadi

DARING TO DREAM

Lucille Mandin PhD

As an education professor at a francophone faculty, I was chosen as a Canadian representative for a five-week program in Ouagadougou, Africa. We were delegates exploring Second Language Pedagogy practices in French-speaking countries of the world. This would be my first trip to Africa and the first time I travelled solo abroad, leaving my husband with my 20-month-old son.

At first, I thought this was impossible, given my family situation. However, a few of my colleagues convinced me this was feasible. They volunteered to support my husband with the care of my son on weekends. This decision was not an easy one to take. Would I choose the right words to help him understand my deep desire to discover the world? Firstly, I had always dreamed of travelling to Africa. Furthermore, it was a professional opportunity that was difficult to refuse. Finally, I believed this would be a good opportunity for my husband to spend quality time with our child. Despite all the challenges to share my reasons to lean towards accepting the offer with my husband, I accepted the opportunity.

Another unexpected dimension appeared in the context of my decision. My beloved father, who was very discrete when it came to my marriage, shared his concern. He told me, "When a woman has a child, she has a responsibility." So, I had to confront my patriarch whom I loved so much. I do not know where I found the courage to take a stand with him. I calmly told him, "Papa, there are things that we don't learn in books. Some things must be experienced." I came to understand my father was afraid for me, as a woman travelling alone in Africa. This was one of the first times in my adult life I had to take a leap of faith. I had to trust all would unfold well.

Although I was travelling as a university delegate, there were many unknowns in travelling to Africa. I had to embrace the ambiguity of not knowing. Once I had decided, I fully committed to taking advantage of this cross-cultural experience as an educator but also as a citizen of the world. I knew there was something for me to learn. I had to trust that I could navigate the system.

On the aeroplane, I read there was a political situation brewing where some African extremists in Burkina Faso were discontent with the colonizers of the country. As a White, female francophone tourist, I suddenly felt very targeted. I can still remember landing in Ouagadougou at 5am; the sun was rising but it was already very hot and humid. As I came off the tarmac, I was met with security guards carrying military guns. Quite a daunting welcome for this Caucasian young woman, travelling alone, venturing into the unknown!

On arrival at my hotel, I was told not to eat any raw foods or anything that was washed. Therefore, no salads! When I saw people selling meat in the streets, raw unwrapped cuts of beef on their arms, which people unwittingly touched with their hands, to decide if they would buy it, I chose to go to a vegetarian diet. I ate a lot of pasta, omelettes, and French fries and drank wine and warm soft drinks (no ice) with most of my meals. I brushed my teeth with bottled water. The heat was very challenging for me. I had to adapt very quickly to new foods and a new schedule.

As we gathered with the other delegates for the first time, I realized I was one of two White people, and I was one of three women in the delegation. Given the context and the common professional goals, we soon got to know each other. One can imagine the diverse conversations around our respective realities! I socialized with African colleagues, many of them were Muslims, and some of them were polygamous men. In five weeks, my view of the world was transformed. I felt like I was in a National Geographic magazine moment. I quickly understood the privilege I had to discover francophone cultures in Africa, in such an authentic and organic way.

Although I had been a professor for a certain number of years, I became aware of the challenge of using my voice in that professional space. As a woman, it felt very different speaking my truth in this culturally and professionally diverse context. In private conversations, we exchanged our realities, and I was privy to how systems work in different cultures. This experience raised my level of consciousness regarding morals and lifestyles. When I left Ouagadougou, I knew I would return to Africa, though I did not know how or when.

Indeed, I did return to Africa, with university students. I accompanied eight cohorts of students in Kenya, Tanzania, and Togo from 2009-2016. It was during those educational and humanitarian annual three-week projects that I created long-lasting relationships with some African women. Following my first solo trip to Africa, I did not hesitate to accept the academic assignment to lead leadership and educational programs in Africa. I was so excited to bring students to discover what I had experienced. It was indeed a life-changing experience. I fell in love with Africa.

Over time, I fell in love with these women. We were able to share our lives and I connected with them. We talked about the realities of being in a polygamous relationship and their experience of female genital mutilation practices, topics so foreign to my lived reality. When I was invited into African women's homes, I understood what an honour it is to have the privilege to enter someone's private space. We connected on a deep level, opening the opportunity for authentic, intimate talks. I was able to create relationships with them where we trusted each other.

When I retired, I wondered, *What do I do with the rest of my life? What is my greatest gift to give? I'm vibrant, I'm healthy and young.* A few years ago, I was invited to join a global women's group, Global Institute for Evolutionary Women (GIFEW) where I discovered I wanted to continue to contribute in whatever way I may be called to do so. Within months, with the support of GIFEW women, I pursued my dream to create a foundation to empower African women. I felt compelled to support these African women. In 2020, I created a charity, *Hand-in-Hand with African Women,* to empower them to create sustainable structures to help them become autonomous and self-reliant. Little did I know this first solo voyage in Burkina Faso, would open the door to becoming a change agent for restorative and social justice.

Today, we work with three African communities who are developing enterprises of their own. Very soon, those women will have their income and they will be able to support whatever projects they embrace. It is time for me to 'give back' because the universe has been so generous to me. I know that I created my life. I want women to have opportunities to experience freedom and choose powerfully to embrace what matters most to us.

The biggest thing I learnt from my solo travel journey is trust. I had to trust I was making the right decision. I had to believe in possibilities and then embrace ambiguity. This was already part of my personality, but going to Africa, I said to myself, "You know you are going to encounter very new things but just stay open to possibilities." Finally, graceful audacity emerges as a value to move me forward despite my fears and my hesitations. These lessons served me well to embrace solo travelling. Daring to dream was so worth it! This is a message I would like to share with women.

My three tips for an aspiring solo female traveller:

1. Be curious: Do your research - Learn as much as you can about the context where you are going. Make sure you pack wisely; it is important to be comfortable.
2. Be wise: Get good insurance so that you're protected if something happens. Keep your emergency numbers accessible and inform people of your plans.
3. Be brave: Venture out as much as you can. Carpe diem, seize the moment and live it to the full.

Lucille Mandin PhD, is the founder of Hand-in-Hand with African Women, a charity whose vision is to empower African Women. She is a retired professor from the University of Alberta, who has touched countless lives and has created ripples across the planet. She continues to bring the spirit of empowerment to everyone she meets, inspiring them to develop abilities and talents that benefit others.

Website: www.handiinhand.space

NURTURING AUTHENTIC CONNECTIONS

Dr. Ambika Sampat

In 2007, I had just gotten approval to start my PhD program in the field of Gynaecology & Obstetrics in New Zealand, where I lived with my family. The first of the three-year programme entailed standardization and setting systems, and to get all that done felt like a huge win. With my first year coming to an end, a curve ball was thrown my way as my PhD supervisor, one of the leading experts in New Zealand in Placental Research, announced he got offered a director role at a leading obstetrics hospital in Perth, Western Australia, and he'd accepted the offer. A big accomplishment for him, but that meant I would be left with no supervisor!

He offered me a full scholarship to move to Perth and continue my PhD under his supervision. The thought of moving to Perth occurred to me as unappealing as it was one of the most isolated places in Australia. Moreso, the research facility in Perth was a brand new one, which meant we would need to build all the systems from scratch and set up the entire laboratory there for the work we did.

I had never envisioned leaving New Zealand in my life planning. I always thought I'd leave my 'parents' nest' when I got married; the cultural norm for us. This move was disruptive not only academically, but emotionally and socially too. My dad's initial response was to depart from the PhD path and stay back. He suggested I seek another supervisor in Auckland and start a whole new project afresh, which I was not at all interested in doing.

I bit the bullet and mustered up the courage to pursue my education. I didn't realise it then, but it was a total interruption of the cultural pattern I was brought up in, coming from a family where women got married in their early 20s and only left their parents' home when they did. There I was, packing my bags to go across the ocean to pursue a doctorate, solo. As heartbreaking as leaving my closest bonds was, my parents and grandparents ultimately supporting my choice gave me the courage I needed for this unfamiliar and very uncomfortable adventure ahead.

Many of my friends had travelled solo and the majority chose to do so. Moving into a new country and territory came with joy, excitement, curiosity, and discovery for them. I had none of that. All I had was fear.

I moved to Perth in January 2008, and it was an adventure and discovery in every way possible. I had never rented a place on my own before, bought upholstery, or travelled to a super remote, isolated place by myself. It was scary and daunting. On my first night, I sat in bed and sobbed inconsolably for missing home. The following morning, I felt a new possibility kicking in as I made my way to the new hospital where I would go on to spend the next two and a half years of my life and create some of the most remarkable memories to date.

King Edward Hospital was the largest maternity hospital in Western Australia. What I had thought was going to be a major step back in my doctorate timeline turned out to be one of the greatest growth and mastery opportunities for me by training alongside world-class experts in the field of placental and foetal research.

In New Zealand, I was in a well-established, internationally acclaimed, leading research centre, The Liggins Institute. I was one amongst many — unseen and buried in the crowds. In Australia, the exposure to working with an intimate team of industry pioneers whilst designing and creating an entirely new maternity biomedical research facility at this well-established hospital was incredible. The standardization and systems set-up for my research took about seven to eight months, and contrary to my initial perception, that process turned out to be of the most profound learning experiences one could face in medical research.

The years that I spent in Perth were perhaps the first phase of my becoming the woman I am today. From a personal perspective, I immersed myself in different social networks and expanded them in ways I'd never imagined. I didn't know anybody there before I went and I got to see how versatile and how adaptable I was in new environments, which was a pleasant surprise.

Growing up in Zambia and then New Zealand, I was gifted a large social circle through my parents' wonderful lifelong friendships; their friends' kids became my lifelong buddies. We lived across continents together and surfed across the beautiful phases of childhood, teens, and 20s together. As blessed and joyful as that was, what I didn't realise was, in those safe comfortable networks, I never got to discover who I was. I had a set perception of myself — and it was finite.

Moving to a new country gave me a blank canvas to discover myself and my likes and dislikes. I created friendships that were new in every way possible — and they were amazing. I could show up in any way I wanted to; there was no limitation to how and who Ambika could be. No past reference. No past limiting identities. I learned that I love playing the drums and did a 10-week course and played the entire drum kit, which I enjoyed. I love dancing, and as a kid, I did numerous dance performances at large social events, which went out of existence in New Zealand and then got reignited in Perth.

I never knew I enjoyed adventure in New Zealand. I had never remotely related to trekking, and in Perth, I discovered how much I enjoyed being in the outback, kayaking and trekking. I was learning so much about myself, and it felt like I was in a bubble my whole life up until then, and the bubble finally popped, and I was getting to spread my wings.

One significant decision I made because of this experience was in my final seven months, I set up a non-profit platform with my best mates. The whole notion of 'social enterprises' was budding in the early 2000s, and I learnt about it from my then-boyfriend now husband, Ronnie Sampat.

He was based in the UK and did a 10-day immersion journey with a non-profit organisation in a rural part of west India. There, he bought 1000 handmade greeting cards made by kids from slums, through an organisation called Manav Sadhna that empowered children to tap into their talent to generate revenue and disrupt the culture of charity and donations. The whole concept was so inspiring, I asked Ronnie to send me a box of 500 cards. My best mates and I went on to create a project over a few months, where we set up stalls across the city of Perth after hours and promoted the work of the talented Manav Sadhna children. This was something I'd never done before, none of us had, and the capital we raised was then invested in another charity. From one to another, we set up our first non-profit platform, iNUT-Who? (If not you then who?), to bring awareness to people on new effective and more impactful ways of making a difference.

With that seed planted in my heart, as I completed my PhD and relocated to London to start my first job as a Postdoctoral Fellow at King's College, my heart felt it didn't belong in the biomedical world anymore. I chose to transition careers, park aside the attachment to the 'doctor' title and all society-accepted perks it comes with, and instead work in the development and impact investing sector for the next eight years, where I travelled globally, became an international speaker across multiple platforms, and created a greater social impact. A significant departure in my career based on what I discovered about myself in Australia.

My one defining moment from my trip to Australia was the night I had a real big breakdown in my relationship of six years (long distance), it felt like it was coming to an end. I was heartbroken, I felt extremely vulnerable, and was up all night. I called one of my best mates at that crazy odd hour, and within minutes, in those early hours of the morning, she showed up at my doorstep with my two other best mates. They nurtured and looked after me, and we did whatever we needed to do together. This, and many other such moments like working late in the hospital and them driving by to drop off meals, granted me the true gift of deep friendship. Such moments in Perth brought awareness of how much love, loyalty, and commitment I have invested in my friendships, and the exuberant rewards. The return on investment is multiple folds more. I had so many moments of belly-hurting laughter during my stay in Perth, memories that still bring a smile to my face a decade later. These bonds have transcended geographical and time barriers; we seem to grow closer as we age, a testament to the power of harnessing and nurturing authentic connections.

My three tips for an aspiring solo female traveller:

1. Commit to self-discovery through immersion in diverse environments. I continue to discover myself more through continuously immersing myself in different communities. Having lived across four continents, and travelled to 30+ countries, I have learned that human beings are the same. Although we have some man-made differences that exist only in language, everyone speaks one common language of love. Everyone yearns to belong. You will discover the best of human beings when you go beyond superficial differences and immerse yourself to seek and celebrate the similarities. So, do it more. Don't hold back.

2. Allow yourself to flow when you're travelling. Flow in this context means to give up any attachment to your likes and dislikes. Free your mind from self-resistance. Open yourself to discovery in the new land, culture, and traditions. I have learned so much about letting go and adapting to the flow of the environment. Letting go has produced new bridges and an ocean of wisdom.

3. Capture your memories in a 'gratitude journal.' A guaranteed way of enjoying life is by training the mind to pro-actively identify what you're grateful for daily and documenting it. The more you get to do that, the greater abundance and joy you experience. Try it!

Dr. Ambika Sampat, Director at FITBANKER, an organization specialising in healthy lifestyle coaching, leadership development, and adventurous experiences. With a Doctorate in Obstetrics & Gynaecology, Dr. Ambika combines a medical background with a passion for unleashing human potential. Her expertise extends to leading relationship and leadership coaching programs, driving investor engagement across Europe, and resource

Vaishali Patel

mobilisation in developing markets. An international speaker in various sectors and geographies, Dr. Ambika is dedicated to inspiring individuals to lead fulfilling lives while prioritising health and well-being.

Website: www.fitbanker.com/hr
Instagram: @dr.ambikasampat

I CAN BE ON MY OWN

Wendi Matthews-Ortiz

Most of my travelling alone was because of my job as a flight attendant. It seemed to be the obvious career for me as I wanted to travel the world and satisfy my sense of adventure and curiosity.

One of my most memorable trips as a flight attendant was when we travelled to Hong Kong. My company was hired to return refugees that had been on a boat that was trying to attempt to come to the US. The boat was stopped just below California and never made it to the port of the US. Our company flew on a DC 10, which was at the time, one of the larger aircraft's that was available to pick up these refugees.

This trip was probably the most eye-opening and enlightening. I remember witnessing what these refugees thought an aeroplane was and what they were told would happen to them if they took off their seatbelts. I realised that there are a lot of people in this world that are very sheltered and don't know what it's like to live in a world where having an aeroplane or being able to get in a car is an everyday thing. Some of the things that these guards that were travelling with them were telling them, I was appalled by. It just made me reflect on how lucky I was to live where I did, and that privilege was something that I was born with. I did have the privilege of travelling.

We dropped the refugees off in China and we were not allowed to look out the windows. There were guards at the bottom of the stairs with machine guns, and I felt my heart ache for those people. It made me want to have a better view of what other parts of the world look like. We ended up staying the night in Hong Kong, and instead of doing what would be the normal tourist thing to do, I joined the pilot and a few others for dinner in a poverty-stricken part of Hong Kong.

I attempted to communicate with the locals, and they were so gracious, kind, and caring, despite the language barrier. The conversations were simple, and they were accommodating. We went to a restaurant and my big thing was, "Don't tell me what I'm eating. Unless I like it." I tried different local dishes and most of the time, I had no idea what I was eating. The one thing that I did not try, and I haven't even looked on, was monkey brain, which is a delicacy there!

It was eye-opening to learn from the locals and realise that the rest of the world doesn't live the same way we do. That was probably one of the trips that prompted me to start to dig into places, to go be part of the community and meet the people, not just to do the tourist thing. In Hong Kong, I didn't make any lifelong friends because there was a communication barrier, but I started to change the way I travelled.

I realised from this trip that I love people and I always have. I developed compassion around someone's situation, and I like to pride myself on not being a person that judges others. I was in a country that I was ignorant about, and I chose to educate myself on the culture and customs. This stayed with me when I went to different countries, and it was interesting as each place was very different.

One of the things that I started to appreciate was just being by myself. I love to be around other people, but I found that when I would go to New York, I would go to the same restaurant outside of Central Park and I would sit outside by myself and have a glass of wine, just to be by myself. If I talked to someone, great, but it was not like I needed to. It allowed me to just take in everything around me. It always freaks people out because I would venture off by myself, but for me, it gave me peace. I could connect better with who I was.

Working as a flight attendant was an escape for me because I was in an abusive marriage at the time, and I would purposely choose flights where I would be gone for 60 days at a time. It was my way of escaping reality, and it was healing for me to know that I can be on my own. When the reality of it being time to get out of the abusive marriage came, I knew that I could do it because I had been travelling by myself. I had been taking care of myself and had lived in the Cayman Islands for six months without anybody taking care of me. It was an escape for me, and I learnt that I can be on my own and I can do this. Probably for the first time in my life, I realised that about myself.

My trips helped me to understand myself better and to ask questions of myself. I reflected on what I was learning from various cultures and my life. When I went to Germany, it took me a long time to find the Holocaust Museum because everybody that I asked denied that it even existed. It was eye-opening for me to witness that there are things that happen in our world that people pretended like they never even happened. I could understand why the Germans would feel that way. But it was part of their history, and it did happen, so it's not like they can hide from it. It made me reflect on and think about what I have hidden and denied and not owned in myself.

I think there were moments during my solo travels when I was afraid. One such time was when I went to Bahrain. A woman or group of women travelling in the Middle East is not unusual, however, at the time, it was well-known that a woman who is fair, has light-coloured eyes, and is American was something to be concerned about. We were warned to not go out alone and certainly not without being covered, as I was a potential target. Although I am fearless, I listen to warnings and concerns while I travel. I respected the culture and would dress as the locals and abide by their requests for women to cover their faces. I travelled in the late 90s, which was a popular time for a young woman to be approached to come live on a commune and make a prince's paid concubine. You'd become part of his harem. I was not approached but I did have friends that joined and luckily for them, they came home safely after a few years.

Throughout my years of travel, I chose to learn and abide by the local cultural preferences and customs to stay safe. One rule that I didn't abide by was when I and a couple of other crew members decided to try and make the guards at Buckingham Palace laugh. We did everything we could to get them to laugh. They didn't budge, crack a smile, or blink. It amazed me. The people around us were laughing. Right before we left, we caught one who'd begun to smile, but I often think it was more because we were walking away than what we had been doing.

My three tips for an aspiring solo female traveller:

1. Don't hold back. Do all the things you want to do. Don't let fear hold you back from trying something new or talking to a stranger.
2. Live as a local. If you're staying in a hotel or hostel, go and be with the local community. It's a great way to discover people and you never know who you might meet.
3. Share yourself with people. Don't just be one-sided. Take the time to learn about their culture and share who you are because, most likely, they want to know you too. Many people can't travel but you can share your life with them, and where you're from, and they can still get that sense of who you are and know where you're from.

Wendi Matthews-Ortiz is a Private Jet Broker, best-selling Author, Coach, Speaker, and world class transformation leader who helps people awaken their potential and start living a life they love through gaining clarity, personal power, and forgiveness.

Website: www.harwenconsulting.com
Instagram: @wendiortiz_celebratepassions
Facebook: wendi.matthews.9
LinkedIn: wendi-matthews-ortiz-505479/

DISCOVERING MY CREATIVITY

Pooja Gandhi

Travel was not just a passing phase for me; it was an intrinsic part of my family's DNA. My parents instilled in us the value of hard work and exploration, and they were a living demonstration. They worked hard, saved money, and took my brother and me on thrilling adventures that nurtured a strong bond between us.

As I grew older, I found myself questioning my identity and place in the world. High school years were tough; I didn't fit into many groups and felt like a bit of a loner. My unique lifestyle and perspectives gained from extensive travel led to differences in interests and misunderstandings with fellow students.

Six months after my graduation from university, I yearned for a fresh start, far away from familiar faces, where no one would know who I was. A close friend had moved to Cambodia and opened a restaurant, fuelled by creating a new life for himself. I was inspired by him and longed for something beyond the confines of commercialism. Having travelled to India multiple times before, braving the challenges of third-world countries, I embraced the adventure to Cambodia without fear.

One such adventure in India that I felt prepared me strongly for Cambodia was witnessing an accident on a busy street in Jaipur. It was a really hot, sunny day and there was a ton of traffic. I got annoyed and short-tempered. I got out and went to see where the accident was and realised it was on the sidewalk. A lady had died, and people had gathered around while others walked over her. I strolled over to her, and after taking a few steps, realised that I had just walked over someone. I had no empathy or disregard for the fact that she existed. I realised at that moment that I almost felt a bit desensitised.

The Lonely Planet book covers the region and people who have travelled around Asia extensively. They say not to give money to beggars, and I wasn't prepared for what that would be like in traffic. Being constantly asked for something as a tourist, such as, "Can I have this?" "Give me this," "Do this," I started to become desensitised to that side of giving. I was confronted with my own desensitization, realizing how easily I had walked past a person in need. This awareness made me leave India – I didn't want to become that person who could not feel compassion.

I went to Cambodia with my eyes and heart wide open. In the six years that I lived in Asia, I worked for a year and then would go travel for two to four months at a time. Cambodia was like my home base from which I travelled around Southeast Asia. Teaching English is a good option for a lot of people who want to make some money when they're travelling. I taught English for a couple of hours a day and noticed that a lot of us in the ex-pat community couldn't fit into Asian-size clothing. We would have to go to Thailand to do clothing runs.

I had thought that as I was in the garment manufacturing capital of the world, I would open my store and design and sew clothes. I hired local women and opened the store with my partner at the time. We taught the women English, and they taught us the local language so that we could give them designs. We did well, and it turned into a self-running shop where we exported clothes for a while. That was how I made my money, and I was able to pay off my student loans. On my return home, I didn't have much money, but I didn't have any debt either.

I loved getting in touch with my creative side by designing clothes. I never had an artistic upbringing or any artistic interest. I was a numbers person, a finance major, and a little bit dry in that world of being creative. It was interesting to me that I had stepped into this world of design. An introvert like me would never show my designs in North America and ask people what they thought. I was never that free and bold nor did I have that innate inspiration or courage. In Cambodia, I didn't have that fear. It is such a big part of what defines who I am today.

I tried so many new things in Cambodia. I went on many adventures such as bungee jumping and adventure sports to taking the time to learn the language of Cambodia. I invested time in understanding the local language, and in doing that, it opened entire worlds for me. It is the rules of engagement between a foreigner and a local person, in the sense that they suddenly look at you and treat you differently. When I go somewhere now, I spend a lot of time beforehand learning the language, because I recognise that it helps to build connections with people when you show that level of interest.

I did come to a crossroads in my life, and I made a lot of bad decisions in Cambodia. I had access to a lot of drugs, and I had no responsibilities or anyone to be accountable to. A lot of my mistakes came from being drug-induced and abusing drugs. I think that's a part about travelling that maybe we don't speak about much. When I came back to Canada, I got a lot of help in healing the past. It was a part of my past that offered me so much value and experience. I had decided in Canada to reconnect with my family and my brother. I had to take an intentionally disciplined approach to look at some of my behaviours. I couldn't do that in Cambodia.

Having exposure to various cultures and embracing norms, I had to adapt to cultural rules on the fly. It enhanced my social intelligence and ability to be very aware of common, unspoken rules of humanity. It's as simple as acts of kindness or acts of recognition. It allowed me to be very intuitive to the environment and be able to adapt and read a room without understanding the language — through body language.

The most beautiful thing travel did for me is give me the courage to be okay with being alone. That's my proudest achievement. I've raised my son alone since birth and I'm still very much a loner in many ways. I have a lot of peace with that because I recognise that I'm never truly alone.

My three tips for an aspiring solo female traveller:

1. Find the land and let the universe take you. Lose the map. Let the people be your guide. Never in my travels did I ever carry a map, and it never failed me. I always found my way and I learnt a lot by being an adventurous spirit.

2. Embrace the quiet of being independent and not having to tailor your day, needs, or wants to someone else's schedule, needs, or interests. There's a lot of freedom that comes from doing what you want to do in a new place. I appreciated that more than anything because when you fast forward and you have children and family commitments, everything is about what somebody else wants to do.

3. When you get to travel and have an opportunity to do exactly what you want to do; there's a lot of freedom.

Pooja Gandhi is an experienced and thought-provoking strategic leader. With over 10 years' experience in operations, she has leveraged her experience traveling abroad to improve and drive company growth all while furthering her education and being a mom to her son, Everest. Pooja graduated from the University of Alberta in 2004 with a Bachelor of Commerce in Finance and most recently has completed her MBA with the Australian Institute of Business.

STRONG, INDEPENDENT WOMAN

Katherine Longhi

It was 1996 and I was 16 years old when my French teacher asked, "Who wants to go to Europe?" My hand shot up immediately in response. I was the only one in my class, so my parents paid for me to go to Paris and London with students from another school. The European trip was a sweet 16th birthday present for me from my parents, which is a big age in America.

When I arrived in Paris, I promptly burst into tears in front of the iconic Eiffel Tower. This is one of my most memorable moments from all my travels. I'd seen the famous Parisian monument in my French book and here it was, right in front of my eyes. I believe creating something in your mind and then seeing it in real life makes you think that anything is possible. Seeing something with my own eyes was a transformational experience. It was my first solo travel trip without my parents, and I was outside of my comfort zone being with kids I didn't know from a different school. That trip set me on my path to be a lifelong traveller and adventurer. I learnt that anything is possible. I can read something in a book and experience it by creating a plan to make my dreams come true.

A year later, another opportunity came up to travel to Rome, Paris, and Madrid. I asked my parents if I could go, but they said, "No. We can't pay for another trip to Europe. Are you crazy? What teenager goes to Europe twice in two years?!" It was then that I decided at 17 years old that no one was going to tell me what I could or couldn't do. I borrowed 1500 US dollars from a friend. It was an astronomical sum for someone who worked

20 hours a week on minimum wage at the mall. I told my parents, "I'm going. I borrowed the money from Carla. Bye!"

This trip was the first one I had generated for myself through working and fundraising. I told myself, "I'm going to do whatever I want to do and go wherever I want to go. I am my own strong, independent woman." It was a crucial decision for me as a teenager growing into adulthood.

One experience I had on this trip profoundly changed me forever. One night, I had an adventure with two girls on the Spanish Steps in Rome. Instead of listening to our tour guide outside the Trevi Fountain, we decided to venture off. Sitting on the Spanish Steps, two German boys sat next to us, and we had conversations about history that made me think of American history.

What they said to us in that conversation surprised me. It wasn't long after the fall of the Berlin Wall, and they said, "We're so sorry, we're German." We said, "What are you talking about? Why are you apologising for being German?" and they said, "Well, you must hate us." I had no idea what these boys were talking about. In the United States, our world history education rarely makes it to World War II unless it's at the university level. At this point, I hadn't had that education yet.

It profoundly shaped me to open my eyes outside of America, and that history gets embedded in the DNA and culture of others. There's so much healing that needs to happen. I felt it was unfair that the German boys had to carry around guilt from what their ancestors did over 50 years prior. I got interested in other people and their history. I said to myself, "It doesn't have to be this way."

When we got back to the group after that conversation, we were shunned for sneaking away and talking to boys. I told them everything the boys had told me, and the other kids told me, "That's their stuff," to which I replied, "Well, I think we're better than this." I was shocked by what I was hearing. For me, Americans became insensitive to the extent of not caring about other people. After that, my intention was clear. My American Dream became My European Dream, and I would do whatever it took to get back to the Old World. Through this trip, I saw that I had become an independent young woman who could fulfil her plans. If I want to go to Europe, I'm going to go to Europe, and I'm going to find a way to make it happen.

In 2000, as part of my university degree (European Studies, no surprises there!), I spent the year aboard in Bologna, Italy, and Grenoble, France. In Italy, I had my first serious boyfriend. He was Italian and we spoke Italian with all of our friends. I was finally able to be myself in a foreign language. I had Italian friends whom I had a deep level of relatedness with beyond the experience of most foreign exchange students. This again gave me access to other people's authenticity and culture. It just propelled me to get back to Europe. During my time living in Italy, the love and the authentic friendships made me who I am today.

After I graduated from university in New York in 2002, I worked at Bloomberg. I told my colleagues and anyone that would listen that I wanted to return to Europe. On my 23rd birthday, I was lucky to spend the day in London with my colleagues. When I returned to New York, I was in a lift when the Global Head of Recruitment asked me, "Hey, what did you do last weekend?" and I answered, "I went to London for my birthday. Doesn't everyone go to London for their birthday?"

A week later, the same recruitment lady called me into her office with the CEO. She said, "Hey. I remember you liked London a lot. Would you like to live in London?" I didn't hesitate or need to think of the implications. I responded immediately in the affirmative. The recruitment lady continued, "Okay, great. We've got a job there. You'll be managing 40 people in customer service, and you'll go as soon as we get you a work permit." In 2003, I had a one-way ticket to London.

On June 30, 2003, I met a man in my department who is my husband now. We got together later that year. He's just what I always wanted, a tall, dark, handsome, and funny Italian! Bloomberg gave me a wonderful community that I'm connected with. I got to travel a few times a month for work. I thought that I was living the dream. Year after year, seeing the insides of airports, taxis, conference rooms, and offices made me realise that this wasn't the way to enjoy travelling.

In 2012, I took my first solo trip. I was making a big career pivot from finance to catering and I wanted to celebrate. None of my friends wanted to come with me to travel because they had things planned. I went to Barcelona, the best city in Europe to live in, and it was the first time I was travelling without anyone to meet on the other side. I felt that I needed to do it. It was like a kind of rite of passage, with no itinerary and no one to meet. The experience was empowering for me because I usually travel in groups. I decided that when I next travel on my own, I would be intentional and create what I want to get out of it rather than just go solo travel because no one else could travel at the time.

Since COVID, I have considered London as my home base. I had lockdown travels (1-3 months at a time) to Florida, Northern Italy, Calabria, Dubai, and Cyprus. My husband and I spent more time with our family during COVID than in the previous 20 years added up. It was heaven! After a few decades of leaving our families behind to travel the world, I realised that home is where my family is. The COVID years have given me an entirely new way of travelling which is more like extended travelling or short-term living. The experience has given rise to a new dream of mine — to split our time equally between Italy, London, and Florida on an ongoing basis.

My travels taught me to care for every history — becoming interested in other people's languages, going to foreign lands, and becoming a global citizen and eventually a changemaker. It's my career now to grow and develop women. I'm constantly looking for new cultures and diversity to bring to our constellation of evolving women.

My biggest fear about travelling is always the fear of it being over. I was afraid of being stuck in places that I didn't want to be and missing out on going places where my soul is happy and free. The fear of not getting back to Europe, Italy, and London. The fear of not continually creating those experiences in the trips themselves, having no plans to go anywhere, and no possibilities. Freedom is a huge value of mine (not just because I'm

American), so feeling like it is threatened is a huge deal for me. An easy way to not let the fear win is to always have the next trip booked before the current one ends!

My three tips for an aspiring solo female traveller:

1. To dream big.
2. Make a plan.
3. Dance when the plan doesn't go as planned. Plus have fun and don't take anything too seriously.

Katherine Longhi is an international diversity and inclusion consultant, feminine transformation leader, and the Chief Communications Officer at the Global Institute for Evolutionary Women (GIFEW). Katherine coaches women leaders to partner with other women and men to transform society.

Website: https://www.katherinelonghi.com

BEING AN AMBASSADOR

Amy Forsythe

I was on assignment for the US Navy, and I was going to be assigned to Poland for several months to work and live on a new Navy base. I didn't know that the US had a base there, and because it was new, they didn't have accommodation for people to stay on the base as it was being built.

I stayed in an apartment that was rented by the US government in a small town called Redzikowo. It was right on the Baltic Sea in northern Poland. I had never pictured the country of Poland having a beach town or beach lifestyle. People were enjoying the beach lifestyle, sailing, and water sports. It struck me that people are the same; they want the same things, they want a day off to go to the beach and being drawn to the ocean is sort of a universal feeling for people.

I was out in the town living with Polish neighbours, and when I had my weekends free, I would go shopping at the Polish mall and go to the sea. I had an opportunity to go and not just be on assignment and be confined to the base of a military installation. I could live among the local people and make friends there and do the activities that they like to do, which is not unlike where I live, but it just struck me as interesting.

It broke down any fear or ambiguous thoughts I had about what people do in Poland because my image of Poland was World War Two and concentration camps, cold and dreary. I was surprised to find it was vibrant. People were very alive, and the economy was doing well. The people, food, restaurants, and shopping were amazing.

I found the culture and lifestyle in Poland to be like America. People had beautiful homes. It has encouraged me to live there or spend three or four months there in the summertime. The thought of saying I want to go live in a foreign country for three months or more is new to me.

I learned to not have any preconceived ideas about what I thought. Getting first-hand experience on the ground was eye-opening for me, and it kind of broke down any fears that I had about travel.

I felt as if I was an unofficial ambassador for America. That my behaviour and my conduct was going to be very impactful because if Polish people never encountered American people before, I would be the memory that they have of encountering an American. I kept that at the forefront of my mind, reminding myself that I could end up being the only lasting impression that they would have of the country I come from. I wanted to make sure that my interactions were positive, and that if nothing else, they remembered me as being kind and courteous and respectful. I was always on my best behaviour to make sure that was the lasting impression that they had of Americans.

I have my ancestry lineage to Poland, maybe two or three generations back. There are legacy stories that my great, great-grandmother was Polish. It's not a place where Americans go and is certainly off the beaten path of Europe. When I was walking, shopping, or trying to order off the menu, and I was speaking English, I would wonder what people would think — if they thought I could be Polish — but when I spoke, they realised, I'm American.

I did enough research to know that crime in Poland was low. In America, there's always rampant random crime, so you're always on high alert and you always have to look over your shoulder. When travelling to places like Poland, I felt like I didn't have to keep my guard up, as far as crime goes, but you always still have to be aware of your surroundings. I felt that it was sort of a relief that I didn't have to worry about a carjacking or necessarily any random shootings going on at the mall or mental illness. My fears were more to do with getting lost or not being able to find my way or breaking down on the side of the road and wondering how I would communicate with someone who doesn't speak English.

In my line of work, I'm directed to report for duty and to report to a certain address, wherever it may be in the world. I have to focus, find my way, and pay attention to my surroundings and make sure I double-check my equipment and flight details as one misstep and I could be at the wrong location without an interpreter to help me or people who speak English. It could be a very difficult situation at the end of the wrong location, and someone would have to come and find me, and so being self-reliant is important.

Although the purpose of my travel was official military orders, I had to find my way to the base by myself, which was in a very remote location in Poland. Travelling to the airport and the location, renting a car, making sure I had GPS capabilities and navigating with the GPS was all scary because I didn't know if I might have to pull out a map if I lost the signal. I was anxious because I was by myself, and I didn't know where to pull over if something happened. No one greeted me at the airport. I had to make my way to the base, stay in a hotel, and navigate all of this on my own without many instructions. That part was scary because there are not a lot of English directional signs and I had to use my instinct to look at words and see if they were like an English word of where I needed to go.

It was a very nerve-wracking experience to try to find my way by myself to this location. I didn't have a SIM card, so I was just praying on making sure that my phone would navigate me to the place to be so I can link up with people who could help me get to the next place along my journey.

Following my intuition when navigating was important; for example, there are some common themes when it comes to road signs like a no-entry sign, which restaurant to eat at, and which places seem unsafe. Trusting myself and my instincts builds after every trip, and I get to add this to my tool bag.

A defining moment on the trip was when I was on assignment and working as the public affairs officer for this new military base. We had many high-ranking officials, and Polish, US, and NATO leaders come and visit.

The US Ambassador to Poland came to our base and getting to meet the ambassador, and US congressmen and senators, who travelled to Poland to see the space, was pretty special. We escorted them around and answered questions and I documented all of them.

I got to see them do the work they need to in these locations, so they can make informed decisions. Being at the forefront of how policy is made and how people make decisions about budgets and funding and showing them the work of the US military was fascinating because oftentimes in your life, not at the tip of the spear, you're sort of at the lower levels, you're never on the frontlines, seeing how these high ranking, elected officials, or appointed officials who have the highest levels of government are operating and talking with each other.

It elevated my career satisfaction. I was mobilised to active duty as a US Navy reservist and as a Public Affairs Officer. It wasn't my full-time civilian job, but I was pulled to do the Public Affairs Officer role. Sometimes you question, is it worth it. Do I want to do this mission? I was grateful for the opportunity that the US Navy trusted me to be the spokesperson for that job. I accepted the mission and left my home, my husband, and the comfort of my other job to go for this job and it was career-enhancing. Not many people in the Navy get to say they went to Poland on assignment. In American culture, when you can say you're well-travelled, it means a lot.

Looking back at that trip, I realised that even though I was mostly by myself, that I was fine. I didn't necessarily need a travel partner; I was just experiencing it by myself and that was okay with me. I was just taking it in and was able to be more retrospective.

My three tips for an aspiring solo female traveller:

1. Keep a journal! - Take lots of photos and videos of your experiences, but be deliberate about writing what you've seen, what you've eaten, and where you've visited. Record your daily reflections to add context to your photos and review them periodically. This will help you reflect on just how impactful your journey was when you return home.

2. Step off prepared - Research where you're going so you don't feel (and look like a tourist) and you'll feel more comfortable by knowing the history of a particular landmark and the cultural norms of the locals. Study the geography of your travel locations with fold-out printed maps. Also, create a packing list and stick to it! Be discerning about what you're carrying around with you. Start off light to meet strict European weight limits and add to your pack along the way, as needed.

3. Have a contingency plan - Develop your exit strategy in case it's required to evacuate due to a natural disaster, medical emergency, civil unrest, or other circumstances beyond your control. Ensure you have contact information for your country's embassy or consulate nearest you. It's always a good idea and recommended to report your arrival in-country, but most importantly, be prepared to evacuate if needed by knowing where the nearest airport is located and what airlines service your location.

Amy Forsythe is an award-winning military journalist who has been on assignment to several overseas locations, including five combat deployments in Iraq and Afghanistan. She started her career as a U.S. Marine Combat Correspondent and currently serves in the U.S. Navy Reserve as Public Affairs Officer. Amy is the author of the bestselling book titled 'Heroes Live Here: A Tribute to Camp Pendleton Marines Since 9/11.'

Webiste: www.heroeslivehere.com
Linktree: AmyForsythe

WHAT AN ADVENTURE

Marie Soprovich

The story that I would love to share with you involves work, adventure, growth, learning, and leaving my country of origin, Canada. In the summer of 1987, I was in my late 20s and divorced. I had a teaching degree and seven years of experience and since I was new to Edmonton, my teaching contract was a temporary one. I was free! I had a dream that I would be living in a place where there were palm trees and warm weather all year round. This is a story about how that dream came true and just how pivotal it was to my whole life journey.

I remember a hot summer day when I was riding my bike through the river valley, and I heard an advertisement on my Walkman that Alberta teachers were being hired to fill teaching positions in California. I just about fell off my bike and thought, *This is it!* I knew I had to apply for that job, and I knew that if I did, I would get it! Synchronicity is real and the stars are aligned. I applied and even the one-in-a-hundred years, July 27th, 1987, deadly tornado in Edmonton, didn't keep this miracle from happening. It truly was a remarkable day that led to an adventure of a lifetime.

I landed a teaching job in a tough neighbourhood in a city called Compton. The actual city of Los Angeles is not that big and is made up of many surrounding cities such that you don't even realize when you've left one and entered another. It was all new to me. I had never been to LA before and I didn't know anyone other than the principal of the school. Serendipitously, I ended up in Santa Monica, which is a very beautiful part of the Los

Angeles area, and I met people who helped me find my way, including a place to stay. I was fortunate.

I lived in LA for two years and that experience was pivotal. I went there knowing no one, and I knew that, if anything was to be created, it would be coming through me and the relationships and connections that I made. It was a formative and life-changing experience. In many ways, it was a very spiritual journey for me. I just trusted life and knew that my inner source would keep me safe while bringing this transformational experience together.

I had some fear about venturing out into the big wide world all by myself. I faced it head-on and knew that my mind is a powerful creator of my experience. I looked for what was good, and I trusted that! I was always conscious of my safety, but I was also courageous in this bold move. Some people may have labelled this as naive but even though I didn't know everything, I trusted and I took it one day, one hour, one moment at a time. I'm glad about that because had I been too cautious, the adventure would never have happened. Shakespeare said, "Doubt makes traders of us all." Setting doubts aside and going for it is what I said, and I got to know myself through the process.

This was well before cell phones, personal computers, and fax machines! Months went by with very little contact with family and friends from back home. It could have been worrisome but at that time it was just the way it was.

My parents were supportive when I told them I was moving to LA for a working adventure. When I reflect on my family history, my grandparents moved from Europe to Canada, and they didn't know where they were going to end up living and what was there for them. They were adventurous and willing to strike it out to find a new place. They had a lot of faith, were willing to work hard, and trusted life. I felt I was embodying this sense of adventure.

When I moved to LA, I had a job, which was a sense of security for me. I knew I would meet people through work, and I would have income. That grounded the experience for me. I had a purpose and a community.

I didn't return home for a whole year. Then I went back again for another year. In the second year, I was teaching in the Santa Monica/Malibu school district. It was a much shorter commute and a very different demographic. I discovered so much about myself. It was all about finding my way of solving problems, meeting new people, and learning about the diversity of this amazing part of the world where you could be on the freeway next to a Rolls-Royce and a truckload of migrant workers. This is a place where movie stars lived, and homelessness is a huge problem. It was quite something.

There were also so many kind and helpful people along the way who were the answer to my prayers. I marvel at how I managed to navigate this adventure with safety and relative ease. I was so grateful for the adventure of travelling and living in a different culture. The US and Southern California have a somewhat different culture from Alberta, Canada where I was living. One thing that I was present to, was the sense of possibility that existed in LA. Dreams can come true! You can be discovered, and you can discover yourself! That feeling has never left me and I have come to realize that it is not determined by location! LA is a big and diverse place where people often go to seek fame and fortune. For some, it happens. For others, it is the reality of ordinary life. Still, for others, there is heartbreak. The energy is magnetic. For me, it was an outer journey but even more so, an inner journey of self-discovery, the experience of what's possible when one is open to the idea and the curiosity of living one's best life. I wouldn't trade that time for anything.

Two years later when I did return to Alberta, that sense of possibility and "build it and they will come" never left me. I completed my master's at the University of Alberta and continued with my teaching career. The awareness of possibility blossomed into a whole new life for me. To trust in life and face my fears and do it anyway is one of the biggest things I learned from the whole experience. I will not let fear run my life. My practices of mental and spiritual work including affirmations, meditation, regular running, and focusing on the presence of life supported me to embrace the adventure.

When I look back, it was serendipitous that I ended up in Santa Monica. I drove to the end of the freeway which then turned into the Pacific Coast Highway. I hit the Pacific Ocean and knew it was time to get out of the car! Santa Monica is a gorgeous city, and one of the most spectacular coastal cities. I will never forget the day I was driving through this tunnel and suddenly, "poof," the Pacific Ocean was there and the most spectacular beach. For kids from Canada, it was the dream. The beach, palm trees, and people. I parked the car and as I walked towards the ocean, I thought, *I am here. I need to go put my feet in the Pacific Ocean. I can't believe I'm here!* The expansiveness of the experience was magnificent.

I went down to the water and put my feet in the ocean. This gentleman approached me and said, "You're new around here." I asked, "How did you know?" It was probably because I was not tanned and had a Canada tee shirt on but just the same, I sounded surprised that he would pick me out as a newbie! I still laugh at that one!

This gentleman, who was also once a newcomer to America, had the time to enjoy afternoons on this beach. He was friendly and he gave me some good advice. He told me that he owned some apartment buildings and that he and his wife were originally from another country. They had done quite well for themselves. I told him that I had a teaching job and I wanted to find a place to live. He gave me directions about where to look for places to live and on what side of the city was more desirable, and serendipitously, that was how I made my way to find such an incredible place to live.

I met another amazing person a few days later at the beach who also became quite a good friend as time when on. He was just curious about whether I was new, why I was here, and who I was. I chose to be honest and told him that I had found a temporary spot to live, I had a job that started in a couple of weeks, and I was just finding my way around. We went out for dinner that evening and he said he needed someone to watch over his place in Santa Monica and wondered if I would be interested in staying there. He told me that his daughter was in France, the other one was with her boyfriend in Sweden, and his wife had left him for a guy in Hollywood. He had to go back to work up in Sacramento where he worked as an engineer in a nuclear plant.

He told me that he had a little dog that needed tending to and asked whether I'd be interested in renting and looking after his place and his dog for a couple of months. How crazy was that! It was a beautiful place and that's where I lived for the first four months. By the time he and his daughters were moving back, I was able to make connections to find another accommodation that was equally lovely in the Pacific Palisades.

The adventures continued and I would travel to different places in Southern California. My favourite adventure on a Friday night was to get a big coffee from 7-11 and drive around Hollywood and just people-watch and explore. I immersed myself in the culture and observed people, where they went, and where they hung out. I found famous landmarks and I made some friends. I was a long-distance runner then and explored lots of places on my long weekend runs as well. What a time it was!

I also bought myself my first sports car. It was a two-seater, Mazda RX7 with five speeds. Now I had arrived! It was a California car with pop-up headlights and a sunroof, and low to the ground. It was so much fun to drive. I was a real California girl and I loved it!

I had to drive for about an hour on the freeway to get to work. It was part of my spiritual practice, and every day, I would listen to *The Prophet* by Kahlil Gibran. It was a life-changing, spiritual journey for me. I've memorized it and understood every passage. To this day, I can open that book and I know what each of those phrases mean to me and how I see them in my life.

A big realization I had was that life is like a big movie — you get to be your own star, decide how you want to live, choose the script and the things you want to do, and have the adventures you want to have! Being a role model for a life well lived is the greatest gift we can give the world. I am proud of myself for following this chapter of my life adventure.

I would say self-reliance is one of the things that truly strengthened me. I was able to rely on my ability to talk to people, create new friendships, ask for help, and trust myself. There is an energy that resonates and attracts people who are open to exactly what it is that we need in any stage of life. If we are willing to be open to this experience, what we need will show up. The willingness to trust our intuition is so important. That little voice inside that encourages and nudges you to talk to someone, to ask for help, and to believe that the way is shown is so important. Listen to it! We don't need to know exactly how it's going to end; we just need to know that this is our next best step in front of us if we are willing to take it!

Getting to that place of finding a safe place to live, learning the route to work, finding a vehicle and so much more, unfolded in a way that I could never have planned. It was about trusting life, trusting myself to trust that I will be able to navigate life and stay out of harm's way. It was a powerful spiritual journey and an unbelievable life-changing experience.

When I came back to Canada, I wanted to work on my master's and at that time, I met my to-be husband. With that new adventure ahead of me, I changed my mind about the idea of moving back to California. We were both possibility thinkers and staying in that sense of adventure, we started a business together. That whole next chapter of my life was a powerful adventure as well. When my husband passed away in 2012 after a year's battle with cancer, I ended up leaving my education career, because the business now needed a leader. Stepping into that was another parallel journey in many ways because it was a whole new playing field, and my new world and the people in it were in the business community. From an education career to a construction career, leading a company that had a great reputation, finding my way as a leader, and being a role model for others, with a particular focus on women was my new adventure. Travelling solo again! Wow! There were many parallels in this universe.

Again, I had to trust that I would find my way. I didn't need to know exactly how it would all work, but I believed I would find my way as the sole owner and CEO. I also knew there would be people who would support and help in that journey, and they did. I grew to a whole new level of self-reliance and became a leadership role model for women. I worked on committees and boards, and even became the Chair of the Board of Directors for the Canadian Home Builders Association Edmonton Region. That was a big deal as there had only ever been one other woman as chair in the past 65 years. Other women started to step up to board positions and we are still changing the culture in the industry.

The impact we can have when we find our courage, and our ability to step into a bigger way of living, brings the possibility for ourselves and frees others who are watching. If I can do it, so can you! Expand your thinking about what is possible. Be willing to see it another way! Miracles do happen! I truly believe that the experience of going solo to California and having that grand and expansive adventure was character-building and has helped me all my life. I developed the strength to know that I can take on hard things in life, including the untimely death of a beloved spouse and partner. Life is full of challenges, and if I can move through my doubt and fears, so can you! There are some grand adventures just waiting for you. There is so much that is possible for all of us. Embrace it!

It is gutsier and way more fun to say yes to a grand adventure than to say no. Be bold, be brave, and embrace life. That sentiment has launched me over and over again in life. I've now sold the construction portion of my company and am in my third act! I am now the Director of Growth with the Global Institute for Evolving Women. Here we bring transformational education, conscious business, and the aligned power of evolving women together on a global platform! Come and join us and live your best life (www.gifew.com). What an adventure.

My three tips for an aspiring solo female traveller:

1.   Be brave and trust yourself. If you're drawn to travel solo, be smart and be safe, and know that it's doable.

2. Some things are wise to keep in mind and to help you stay safe. Trust your intuition and use your creativity to conjure up what you DO want, not what you DON'T want. Remember, what we focus on grows and our thoughts are powerful. Don't let fear keep you from your dreams. Keep a spiritual practice that grounds you and connects you with your source.

3. Have a little bit of cash or an extra credit card somewhere. Nowadays, it is easy to stay connected but years ago, there was no way to text a friend and tell them you were stuck. There was no GPS or any of the current navigational tools. With a good cell phone, you are never really alone. Still, above all, trust your intuition. The world is full of good people out there who can help and point you in the right direction or give you a little tip or advice. Be open to that and stay grateful.

Marie has a demonstrated history of leadership, education, personal development, business growth, living a meaningful life and having grand adventures along the way! She is an advocate for transformative growth, effective communication and making a positive difference in the world.

Website: www.mariesoprovich.ca
Instagram: @marie_soprovich

JUST GO DO IT

Aruna Paramasivam

My story about my solo travel started in my 40s. I have always loved travel and suffered from a bad case of wanderlust, but it would mostly be jam-packing countries into my limited vacation days and trying to coordinate with friends.

The idea of a sabbatical only became a reality for me later in life. I had acted hard to achieve all my dreams, and I was at the pinnacle of everything that I had wanted to achieve at that point. I had the shiny, glossy life in Manhattan that I always aspired to have. I worked at the largest beauty company, L'Oréal, and I was managing data acquisitions and partnerships for all their top brands. I was doing well overall, and it was everything that I ever hoped it would be. But I realized, as I got closer to the top, that I was feeling quite hollow, void, and unfulfilled; the life I had created was very misaligned with who I was. As a result, there were a lot of things going wrong in that gleaming, glitzy life.

I was getting into a lot of politics and drama at work, and I was finding myself drinking a little bit more wine than I should. Every night, I was taking it out in different ways, and my intuition told me that if I didn't stop, this wasn't going to have a very happy ending. I tried to fit in as many trips as I could with the little time I had but I always felt rushed. I was still checking emails while I was travelling and coming home feeling even more exhausted than when I left, and it never quite felt like the trip I wanted to take.

I finally decided that I was ready to just throw it all away and buy that one-way ticket. It's something that I never had an opportunity to do, even in my 20s, because I was an international student in America. There was no opportunity for a gap year or taking a break because it was all about getting your work permit, your visa, and your green card. I had just gone through all the steps that I should have taken to get to where I was until I realized this amazing opportunity for endless travel was opening up; ironically, because I was now living this life that I didn't want anymore.

My story goes back even before I resigned. I was playing around online, and I found a one-way ticket from New York to Thailand for just $390, and I took it as a sign from the universe. I purchased the ticket first with absolutely no idea of what I wanted to do in Thailand or my life. But I knew if I had the ticket in hand, I couldn't be talked out of the decision. I then resigned from what was considered a very prestigious job and that's how my solo travels started on a large scale in 2018. That trip took on a life of its own. I didn't know where to start. I didn't know that I had picked up some bad lifestyle habits and needed to clear my head. I looked for health fitness resorts in Thailand, and I found this place called New Leaf detox resort. I read all 337 Trip Advisor reviews, and I decided to commit for a month.

I arrived at the detox resort with no other plans but being there for 28 days doing a juice and plant-based smoothie type of diet, exercising, yoga, and meditation to help to clear blocks for me, as well as talking to the people that were also there. It was quite a diverse community as well as a global one and I got many travel ideas from them. That trip ended up being more than six months and I visited 30 countries completely spontaneously.

All my life, I had been a type A personality: needing to do all the research upfront and knowing exactly what I'm getting myself into. On this trip, I didn't take a lot of time to plan. I travelled with an iPhone, and I limited myself to three apps, so I wouldn't get bogged down by information, and I could travel as spontaneously as I could, wherever I felt pulled. It was SUCH a freeing feeling.

After six months, a part of me thought I had enough and perhaps I still enjoyed what I did for a living and just needed a different environment. I decided to join a smaller start-up company in London, which would give me opportunities to travel. But again, once I got back into that life of corporate and back into Manhattan, the lessons I learned didn't quite sink. Six months later, I knew that I had once again not made a good decision, and the opportunity opened again to travel.

It took two or three iterations for me to realize that it was very much my identity that was sunk in my career. Even though I was travelling, I hadn't quite found an alternate identity. Being in my 40s, not having a husband or children, and having only my career, which is where I had thrown a lot of my life, made it difficult to kind of move away because I didn't know who I was without it. That took a little while for me to understand, and I finally decided, one and a half years later, that I was going to cut myself off from all that corporate life for quite a bit and find something else to delve into.

I also wanted a nomadic life. I didn't want to backpack, I didn't want to stay in a hostel, and a lot of the blogs out there are about travelling on a budget. I had decided since I was already in my 40s and I was in a good place financially, that I wanted to travel in a style that was comfortable for me but still conducive to solo travel.

I wanted to find hotels that were boutique hotels, hotels with activities, or hotels that wouldn't be super family- or couples-oriented. I wanted to go to destinations where there'd be other solo travellers in my mindset, my demographic, who were looking to do the same kinds of things that I was.

I wanted to encourage women to explore adventures. I had found myself in my 40s and I wanted to show women that this was the perfect time to start thinking of their next chapter in life. Logistically speaking, for women, the average age of death is somewhere between 76 and 82 — so, in your 40s, you're kind of at the halfway point, and it's a good time to pause and recalibrate, while you automatically think, "Oh my god, am I too old?" "Is anyone even going to talk to me when I travel?" "Am I going to have anything in common with backpackers or the older retired generation?" because you're sort of sandwiched between the two.

I chose not to pursue organising adventure travel trips during the pandemic as I didn't want to be responsible for a group of 15+ people. I pivoted into a coaching business called The Big 40, and it's really for women who want to find themselves or who want to take on a new path in the middle of their life but are wondering if they're too old, or if they've gone down one path too far or too deep and can't quite pivot, or just scared to give up comfort, and don't know if they're able to give up the good for the great. That's really what came up for me on my solo travels.

I travelled to 30 countries in that first sabbatical. I started in Thailand with zero clue. At that time, I just thought I would stay in Asia because I felt like that's where people were doing a lot of this long-term travelling. After all, it's economical, interesting, and easy to get around in the region. I then went to the Maldives, Malaysia, Nepal, Tibet, and Fiji, which was very spiritual. I went to Cambodia and Myanmar, but by the time I reached Cambodia, I felt I had overdosed on temples in Asian culture. I was feeling a little bit of sensory overload and felt I needed to divert my trip.

I remember writing a bucket list with my best friend of crazy things we wanted to do when I turned 40, and one of his had been the Orient Express. A month and a half before my birthday, he said, "Hey, I looked up the Orient Express and there's room on the original route from London to Venice, and it's not expensive. Would you be interested again?" I took that as a sign to leave Asia. My last stop was Northern Thailand, where I took a flight over to London and met up with him, and then took the Orient Express on my 45th birthday into Italy, which brought me into Europe for the second half of the trip. What an entrance in that glitzy ageless train.

In Europe, I wasn't sure what awaited, since it certainly isn't as economical as Asia. I went to Switzerland next, which I was shocked by because it was more expensive than New York City. I then did the Baltics; Lithuania, Latvia, Estonia, and even that — because those countries had switched over to euros — wasn't quite as economical as I had hoped, but I was making my way around. I made it over to Finland, I stumbled upon Bulgaria, and decided that Eastern Europe is where it's at and the Balkans became my favourite part of that trip. I went from Bulgaria, Romania, Serbia, and Cyprus, to Hungary, and at that time, it had been five and a half months and I was getting a little tired.

Once again, I paused and asked the universe, "What's next? I don't want to go home because I don't have a reason to." Randomly, one of my contacts in London was speaking to a company that was looking for someone to lead up their Publisher Data practice in New York, and she threw my name in the hat. I rerouted the trip to go to London to meet with the executives there. After the interview, I flew back to Asia to finish back where I started. I went to Bali and then when I was in Brunei, I finally got the call to say I got the job. I flew back from Macau. I love round numbers. It had been 30 countries in six and a half months and that's what brought me back.

It also stirred a hunger in me because I had seen so many different places and talked to so many different people. I realized after I started my job that the travel bug had not died. That was also another reason that I knew the corporate job had to go because there's only so much vacation you can get with it. It took me a while to let go and I think that was a lesson. I had to learn that there were two more iterations before, and I had to realize that I have the same patterns as before. I was so scared to let go.

That's when I started the coaching business. Now my goal is to try to see as many countries as possible. I have also started this passion for extreme travel. I was just in Iraq, and I flew out on 9/11 on the 20th anniversary just because I wanted that feeling of being empowered to do that.

I learned from my solo travels that despite the differences in all the different worlds that we live in, all women have a fear of getting old, a fear of changing paths, being scared to leave their husbands, scared to leave what they know. I just realized as hard as it was for me to break my patterns, everyone else was, and it was a global issue. That was empowering for me. I also realized there are so many ways of living life like you don't have to attach yourself to a job, an apartment, or a town. It was inspiring to see so many other digital nomads living out their dreams in different ways. I just became confident. I realized I didn't need other people to accomplish what I wanted to do. I could do it by myself, and everything I needed was within me.

I also realized I had suffered from so much information overload all my life and, ultimately, you need to go with your gut feeling, your intuition as they would say, and a few data points to make decisions, not 1000 data points because that just overwhelms you — analysis paralysis.

What started as a sabbatical has become a lifestyle. I travel now. It was me wanting to make an impact on other people's lives through travel and then in the coaching business. In the coaching business, I was able to change someone's trajectory, I was able to influence a person and how they lived, and that was important to me because it was something I wasn't seeing in my corporate job; I'm sure whatever I did had a downstream effect, but it wasn't to one person's life, it wasn't to one present or future, it was very corporate. What I wanted to do was have an impact on people. Show them the opportunities and possibilities, and I was very attached to this 40-something demographic.

One defining moment from my travels was that everywhere I went, people would say, "Oh, of course, you're from New York. You have such a New York attitude." In the beginning, I didn't quite know what that meant. I even took it as a compliment. Then I realised it was a way of being. I saw how aggressive I was, how I needed to know everything, and how I needed to have everything yesterday. I learned to let go, to give up control, and to let go of the need to have control over every outcome. I learned to live a little bit slower. Let things come to me instead of chasing them. Today, I meet people who will say, "What's next?" and I have no problem saying, "I don't know." I have learned to embrace the unknown and be comfortable with the uncomfortable.

Once you figure out how much you want to travel, that's great; you feel great about solo travel, but that raises another question: how long do you want to travel? What is that happy period of being at home versus being on the road? I initially thought, *I don't have a corporate job, let me go out and be a digital nomad. I didn't like that either.* I tried three months in Costa Rica, and I was yearning to go home and sleep in my bed and go to my gym. I realized I am a creature of familiarity and habit.

On my trips, I tried everything new and unplanned. I sometimes have no idea of the destinations or countries I want to visit when I start the journey.

It is very freeing because I am not overloaded with information. I just pick something that appeals to me.

I also have learned to listen to my gut and define what fun feels like. It was not listening to other people's opinions of what they experienced or if this country was dangerous or not great for women as I went with what I could find.

I would go on Trip Advisor and search engines, and I would say this is where I'm going to go, and I would go. Even when I was in the country, I would only decide the day before, or two days before, where I'd go next within the country. Being spontaneous was something I had never tried before. My whole life had been a plan, every day had been a plan. I was a goal setter, I had a to-do list and to give all of that up, and just travel, was something so new to me.

My three tips for an aspiring solo female traveller:

1. Just go do it. You don't need to have things figured out. Don't you dare listen to everybody else.
2. Go with your gut instinct and do your research, but you don't need to have every last fact down.
3. With research, figure out what your happy medium is. Go with your own opinion and don't get side-tracked by other people's opinions. Just because someone else had a bad time doesn't mean you're going to have a bad time there. You could go and have the exact opposite experience, which has also happened to me.

Solo travel allowed Aruna to find her true self and gave her the confidence and resilience to navigate the next chapter of her life. Having been to over 120 countries and all seven continents, she has found joy in each one as she deeply immersed herself in new cultures and found fulfilment.

Facebook: aruna.paramasivam
Instagram: @thearunagram
Linkedin: arunaparamasivam

BEING UNSTOPPABLE

Dr Mandeep Kaur Rai Dhillon

Life was a whirlwind. I met my now husband, Gavin, in 2005, and by 2007, we were married, and our first home post-marriage was London. Shortly after getting married, I was offered an opportunity of a lifetime in Abu Dhabi, which I embraced in the winter of 2007.

One of my biggest worries about being newly married and taking a solo trip for work was about my marriage. It was not a straightforward decision and unconventional for a woman from my culture. Would the marriage work with both of us living on two different continents and having just gotten married? Was this the right thing to do? We were at least a 7-hour flight apart.

We turned the situation into an opportunity for adventure and made the most of the fact that we were half a world apart. We met each other every three weeks in places like Lebanon, Syria, and Jordan. It did wonders for our marriage because it was like constantly being on a honeymoon every two to three weeks in some incredible destinations, staying in some fascinating places, and experiencing a different culture in each nation.

It was just the exact opposite of what I thought the distance would be like. Initially, when I got married, I did what everyone else did — found a place and made a home. Then I made a choice to follow my gut instinct regarding my career, which transported me to a super powerful position. We were both able to enjoy this set-up because we were fulfilled professionally, doing what we wanted to do, and this ultimately helped us bring out the best of ourselves when we saw one another.

It wasn't always smooth sailing balancing an unconventional marriage and an intense career.

A few months before our wedding, I was living in New York and working as a journalist, and I was sent to the Dominican Republic on an assignment. Back from reporting on a story, I collapsed in the hotel lobby. Upon a doctor's examination, it appeared I had lumps in my throat, and despite visiting with several specialist consultants in New York, no one could give me a diagnosis. Hence, my boss at the time, Chad Ruble of Reuters, suggested I return to England and quarantine as I didn't look great.

I arrived back in the UK thinking it was a short trip and I would return to New York. But after a series of investigations at the airport, I was sent to the tropical diseases unit, where I was diagnosed with a rare autoimmune disease called Kikuchis. This is when your body starts to attack itself and is common among Japanese people in their 30s and 40s. I was told to focus on rebuilding my health and to take it easy. That was the end of returning to New York for me, but it was not all bad, because I also took this time out to get married.

Back in London, I had pitched an idea to the founders of Skype, with a university friend of mine, Wilson Chan. Tony Orsten heard the pitch and suggested that I explore a different opportunity at the Venture Capital Fund he was due to join, and this is where I would have the opportunity to change the geo-political dialogue around Islam. I had never visited Abu Dhabi and I was excited. It felt aligned with my faith and the value of standing up for those being persecuted, which I reported on post-9/11. I took the job offer in Abu Dhabi after an eight-month period where I was recovering from my health challenges. The calling was so strong in my gut.

Working in Abu Dhabi was an enriching, fulfilling, and challenging opportunity. I flew to San Francisco to meet with some of the most well-known VC fund managers in the world and was having one-on-one conversations to shape the strategy of the fund — twofour54 ibtikar (which are the coordinates of Abu Dhabi). The opportunity to have that level of exposure was unique. I realised that I was proficient at building relationships and that nothing (such as getting an apartment, paying bills, and finding the right people to work with) was overly difficult when moving to a new location.

I had no idea of the scale of opportunity that would open for me when deciding to follow my gut to Abu Dhabi. I had access to all the money I wanted for this fund. Everyone and anyone around the world were interested, whether it be Silicon Valley funds or the artists across the MENA region in the media sector. I felt as though I could support this position with an MBA.

An executive MBA made the most sense, and I won a place at the London Business School Dubai Campus. Within the school, one student is selected to study at MIT and Harvard; they wrote a strong application alongside achieving top grades. I was over the moon to be selected and it indeed became one of the most rewarding educational and peer group experiences of my life.

What I learned from my solo travel experience to Abu Dhabi is that I'm much more capable in every respect than I ever thought I knew. I went into a brand-new culture and environment, made friends, and walked out with relationships all around the world that are thriving with a lot of respect and love.

The biggest thing I learnt is not to judge. There's a common story about how women are treated with little respect in the Middle East, and yet, I saw that I and almost every other female that I encountered was treated with the utmost respect. In meetings, everyone, especially the men, would stand up when a female walks in.

I learnt to observe without casting judgement. In Abu Dhabi, some men don't get out of their car when they go to their local shop. The shopkeeper comes out and serves them through the window. You can't say that man is being lazy or overly privileged, because you don't know what it's like to walk in the heat of Abu Dhabi. You don't know what it's like to live in that country and culture.

Slowly, I began to realise why things are the way they are. I began to understand the nuances of the culture, for example, how you should talk, when you should apologise, and when you should not question. I had to put aside my linear western worldview to discover and appreciate the culture of another place.

I remember one such cultural nuance that makes me smile. I was attending a wedding in Lebanon, and I decided with my husband that we would meet there. After some extraordinary days at the wedding, Gavin and I were at the airport ready to go our separate ways — him back to London and me back to Abu Dhabi. As we hugged one another to say bye, I noticed a policeman approach us to arrest Gavin. We were both surprised and could not understand why. He then told us that we're not allowed to show public displays of affection. My boss had to come and rescue us from this situation!

Truly, what helped our marriage survive was the fact that we allowed one another to live our dreams. He supported me while he was on gardening leave, to travel to 15 countries in Africa. We had built up that affinity of understanding one another's professional, personal, and spiritual dreams and enabled one another rather than being the barrier.

My three tips for an aspiring solo female traveller:

1. See your gender as an advantage rather than a disadvantage. Strangers may see you and treat you like their daughter, cousin, sister, or friend. Be open to their kindness. Be open to giving as well as receiving — both are important. I found that people treated me very well and I think a lot of that was to do with my gender.
2. Live like a local to experience a place. Stay with a friend or get into the local person's lifestyle. If you're afraid, then know that there are people who will want to support you.
3. Understand that solo travel doesn't need to end once you are married/in a committed relationship.

Vaishali Patel

Dr. Mandeep Rai is a global authority on values, working with companies, institutions, and individuals around the world. She has travelled to more than 150 countries and reported as a journalist for the BBC World Service and Reuters, amongst others.

She began her career in private banking at JPMorgan, and later worked for the United Nations, the European Commission, and grassroots NGOs before setting up the UAE's first media venture capital fund.

Mandeep studied philosophy, politics, and economics (PPE), has an MSc in International Development from the London School of Economics, and completed an MBA at London Business School, with a year at Harvard Business School and MIT. She also holds a PhD in global values.

Mandeep was listed as a 2021 Top Thinker to Watch (Thinkers50) and is the author of The Values Compass: What 101 Countries Teach Us About Purpose, Life and Leadership.

The book is a Highly Commended Business Book of the Year in the DEI (Diversity, Equality & Inclusion category)

Website: www.mandeep-rai.com
Instagram: @mandeeprai
Facebook: mandeep.rai.9847
LinkedIn: dr-mandeep-rai-66b69b3

CHILDLIKE WONDER

C.J. Larson

I am an introvert. I don't often give that appearance because a lot of times people meet me one-on-one, so they think I'm an extrovert and very easy-going. To a certain extent, travelling alone is natural. At the same time, I use the opportunity to push my boundaries, to make sure I introduce myself to new people and things. These new experiences can be life-changing, and I want to share a story of a life-changing encounter with a homeless lady.

In 2010, I had a car accident in LA, and a couple of years later, I had to move back to Oklahoma. I was travelling frequently to California for a legal case. On one trip, I was staying just outside of Beverly Hills, California right across the street from a big farmer's market. It was my first night and I was staying at a new hotel that I was unfamiliar with. I was travelling around the city by bus because I couldn't drive.

Taking the bus system in LA was a whole new world for me. I had lived in LA for almost 10 years, and I'd never taken the bus. I had expected the bus to be dirty, but they were surprisingly clean. I had heard that the bus drivers were grumpy, but they were friendly. The only downside was that I had to anticipate that it was going to take two to three times as long to get from one place to another. The upside is that I met some interesting people on the bus.

One night, I was looking for a particular location to catch the bus and I couldn't figure out where to go next. It was late, just after sunset, and it was getting dark. Suddenly, I heard the voice of a boy behind me, "Are you looking for the bus?"

"Yes," I answered. I turn around, and to my surprise, I saw a homeless woman.

I've always given money to homeless people, and I've bought them sandwiches. But there was something different about this situation. She told me which bus I needed to catch to get to my hotel. She knew exactly where I was going and was incredibly friendly. It turns out, that was her corner. Every time I travelled, I had to pass by her, and over time, I got to know her as a person. It was incredible and turned my mind around about the situation of homeless people.

It's a different lifestyle. A lot of people have thoughts that they're either lazy or just need help. In my conversation with her, she was completely content to live the way she lived. I offered her things I knew, such as where to go to get help, but she was happy and enjoyed how she was living. She said she was living a life of freedom. I was surprised because as a woman, I would feel unsafe and scared living on the streets, but she was totally happy with where she was.

My conversations with the homeless lady made me aware of when I was imposing my beliefs on her. I started to alter the way I looked at people and became aware of where I was coming from assumptions. I used to make assumptions about people based on where they lived and had expectations for who and what they were. Thanks to my experience with this homeless lady, I don't do that anymore.

I don't look at anybody in any way other than what they tell me to believe about them. I don't make assumptions based on appearance, where they live, or how they live. I make an effort to get to know a person for who they are because she showed me that you can't just make assumptions based on appearances. She was an incredible woman.

This encounter was transformative as far as my mentality on how I approach people because I've always been kind of trepidatious regardless of who you are, just because I'm an introvert, but thanks to her, it just kind of helped me break that barrier. I now appreciate everybody's unique and awesome, regardless of their circumstances.

I was in a lot of physical pain from my car accident. I had a lot of worries about whether or not my case was going to be heard or settled. I didn't know if I would have a doctor that could help get me back to normal. After meeting her, I put all that in perspective and I thought, *At least I have a home.* I did have things that I needed to take care of but at the same time, on the grand scale of things, I was far better off than I thought I was.

One thing I took away from my solo travels is to be safety conscious but not paranoid. There's a difference. I don't let fear override anything and at the same time, I don't put myself into a dangerous situation. If there's a dark alley and there are no lights, even though it's shorter to get to my destination, I won't go that way. It's finding that balance in life of being aware and being safe not just for your own sake but for the sake of others.

This also impacts my work as a thesis artist. I work with glass, and I have to think of safety because I work with some toxic materials that can be a safety hazard. I am conscious of that, but also not so focused on it that I don't enjoy what I'm doing. I take the precautions I need to take, and then throw myself into my work with childlike abandon.

My three tips for an aspiring solo female traveller:

1. Believe you are enough company for yourself. Believe in yourself enough that you can be your own company. Some people think they need a travel companion, but you don't. You will be okay all by yourself.
2. Be prepared and plan. If I get stuck in my car, I know who to call and I know places on the way where I can stop. Have somewhat of a plan, but don't try to over-plan. Have a backup battery for your phone and make sure you get your car checked out before you go on a long trip. Do things like that to set yourself up for an amazing trip, so you don't have to think about any breakdowns.

3. Look at everything with a sense of childlike wonder that way, even if stuff is not what you thought it was going to be, there's no room for disappointment. If you get somewhere and think, "This is not what I thought it was going to be," you can still look at it from a sense of, "What can I explore here, and what can I find here that I couldn't find anywhere else?" Spend the time not being critical but truly looking at it with childlike amazement of, "Wow, this is here," even if it's a total dump. It's all in your attitude and how you look at things but bring that childlike wonder, when you're travelling because you will find some amazing things and some incredible places. For example, with the homeless woman I met, once I got over my insecurities, it was wonderful to have an amazing conversation with her, because I didn't try to look at her a certain way, I just talked to her.

CJ Larson is an artist, writer, veteran, kitty mama and foodie. She has had a varied career doing everything from combat correspondent in the United States Marine Corps, to computer programmer, sales, paralegal, and accounting. Currently, she is an award-winning fused glass artist living in Oklahoma. Redefining what it means to be 50, she still travels alone regularly and currently enjoys exploring her home state and the surrounding area, getting inspiration for her fused glass artworks.

Facebook: Blonde Arrow Glass Studio

RE-INVENTING MYSELF

Dr. Shalhavit Simcha

In 2017, I made a life-changing decision to embark on a transformational journey. I was at a festival when I suddenly saw my life from a higher perspective and realised that the next step for me to realise my potential was through a guided structure in the form of a PHD. Having spent almost a decade at Harvard University, I felt stuck in a loop of routine thinking and wanted to break free, grow, and expand my horizons.

When I venture into new places and break away from my routine, it presents a challenging yet transformative experience. Nothing seems obvious anymore, from daily commutes to interactions with others, pushing me to think differently and reinvent myself. This is what happened previously when I had moved from Israel to the US; thus, each move became a stepping stone in my development, allowing me to embrace the choice of being in places where nobody knows me and I can keep uncovering myself.

I created a thrilling adventure to challenge myself and expand my horizons, calling it "My PHD Pilgrimage." My goal was to find a PHD supervisor who would give me the right tools to fulfil my calling. This journey turned out to be nine months in nine different countries, all by myself. I chose to travel solo as when you travel with another person, you inevitably become entwined in each other's world. Sure, the shared experiences and deep connections that can grow are beautiful. However, I learned that even within relationships, it's essential to carve out moments of solo exploration. There's a unique aspect to travelling alone that encourages you to step out of your comfort zone and embrace new encounters.

I chose Northern Europe and explored academic institutions and interviewed supervisors in Scotland, England, Norway, Finland, Germany, Slovenia, Netherlands, Israel, and Ireland. The reason why I chose this part of the world was because when I was a child, my father was away for work a lot and when he returned home, I got to see his blue eyes. I idolised his eyes and thought it would be likely to meet a partner in one of those countries.

I arranged meetings with faculty members at the various universities, and in order to get their time, I offered a free talk on my research projects at Harvard.

I first visited Germany to explore a multimedia university and was delighted to receive a fantastic fellowship offer. However, the offer came with the condition of altering my research to focus on working with young engineering students, which wasn't aligned with my true passion for working with disadvantaged youth. Despite the tempting scholarship, I took the time to reflect deeply on the direction I wanted to pursue.

The next destination was Ireland at a very well-known university in Dublin. I felt very bothered when I noticed that all the students were female and all the supervisors were male in the department I was exploring. When I brought that up to the supervisors who were interested in offering me a position, they contemplated and told me that they had one gay male student. I felt they didn't properly address the inequality issue and I decided to continue my search.

I travelled further south to Cork, where I was blown away by a "queendom." Almost all the faculty members whom I met with and the dean of the university were female and they warmly greeted me. The supervisor who I was most interested in working with, because she was the most attentive and thorough in our correspondences, not only acknowledged and praised my work but also humbled me by suggesting that, for the integrity of my aspirations, there could be something better suited for me elsewhere. I was humbled by her authenticity and care.

A pivotal moment occurred after a relationship in London ended. Seeking solace, I travelled to the University of York as I had read a lot about the research that had been conducted there and I wanted to see the esteemed multimedia department. The Airbnb I had reserved in York messaged me on the day of my arrival, apologising that they couldn't host me but offered to accommodate me as a couch surfer, sharing a room. Being a hippie at heart, I gladly accepted the offer.

During my stay, I met someone at the University of York who mentioned his shy friend, Michael. Intrigued, I suggested we meet him, and the three of us went out together. I instantly clicked with Michael, who had marble blue eyes, and as we spent time together, he mentioned the University of Edinburgh in Scotland, suggesting we go on an adventure there. Interested in the faculty at the business school and film school, I began to contemplate how it could align with my research, which combines psychology and multimedia.

As I explored the University of Edinburgh further, I found myself captivated by Dr Amy Hardie's research on the impact of film. I emailed her and we arranged a meeting. During our conversation, she saw some of my non-academic work. After closing my folder, Amy said, "I want you to express who you are in your research." I was surprised. It was like a cultural clash, a moment of perception shift. At Harvard, I worked tirelessly to make a difference, and suddenly this beautiful human was suggesting that I could express myself in my research. It wasn't earth-shattering, but it made me pause and think, "Wait, can I really express myself in my research? Is that allowed?"

She, being a film professor with a unique perspective from the arts, knew it was hard to convey with words alone. I was moved by this encounter, tearing up as I expressed my eagerness to work with her, even if it meant waiting a year for a scholarship and saying no to the fellowship in Germany. This wasn't the first time I felt inspired by a professor, as moving to the US was also driven by a desire to learn from and work alongside inspiring individuals.

It took almost a year before I was offered a scholarship at the University of Edinburgh to study a PHD in Clinical Psychology. Combining my doctorate in clinical psychology with my passion for music, helped me discover my voice. I create music videos that present my research in a unique and impactful way. By singing my research with words projected on the screen, I've invented a new medium that contributes positively to mental health.

During my entire academic journey, and still today, I often find myself experiencing imposter syndrome. Meeting the faculty in each country was like another mental hurdle to jump over and I often felt anxious.

What would calm me down was connecting to the communities I felt safe with. One such community, which I was introduced to in Boston when studying there, was the Fetish community. I find people are extremely consensual and communicative, which I had never seen on any dating site or even in workplaces. People were so open about communicating their boundaries and desires, and a lot of those desires are not even sexual. People think the BDSM world is very '*50 Shades of Grey*,' but they're endless shades of the rainbow. It was a fun experience, and some relationships were extremely therapeutic.

I cherish the growth and transformation I've experienced through my travels. My journey taught me invaluable lessons, and I'm grateful for the incredible people I've met along the way. I could understand why Ivy League universities consider travel experience in different places around the world could cultivate tolerance and understanding because it provides opportunities to witness people in various situations firsthand. The ability to observe diverse cultures, traditions, and ways of life can lead to greater empathy and a broader perspective.

Here are my three tips for aspiring solo female travellers:

1. Choose a Skill to Develop: While traveling, focus on honing a specific skill and practice it regularly. Embrace the learning process and don't be afraid to fail. Every attempt is a step toward improvement.
2. Embrace Curiosity: People are not intimidating strangers; they are fascinating stories waiting to be discovered. Be curious about

others, notice their emotions, and understand what matters to them. The world becomes a captivating museum of wonders when you open yourself up to understanding people.

3.   Try on New Identities: Traveling incognito grants you the freedom to experiment with different versions of yourself. Embrace this opportunity to become the person you want to be, as nobody knows your past, granting you the chance to practice embodying your ideal self.

Dr. Shalhavit-Simcha is a multi-award-winning PhD researcher, musician, and creative director. Passionate about people's mental-health and multimedia, Dr. Shalhavit-Simcha is the winner of Harvard University's Bok Prize for Public Engagement and founder of PosiFest, the first festival of positive psychology.

Website: www.shalhavit.com
Instagram: @shalhavitsimcha
Facebook: shalhavit
YouTube: shalhavit

I CAN HANDLE IT

Emma Cronshaw

It was 2010, and I was 19 years old. I'd just finished college and had no plans for the future. I wasn't interested in studying anything and didn't know what work I wanted to do. My mum was worried about me and took me to an event for kids who didn't know what they wanted to do. The event had unique and different things you could do after college. The first thing I saw was a company that offered a programme to teach in China. It seemed so exciting and meaningful.

We spent two hours looking at other things at the event but teaching in China was the only thing I wanted to do. I had a good feeling in my gut about it. My parents were surprisingly very encouraging. They knew it was going to be a good experience for me and that I was doing it for the right reasons. They believed that I could do it and they trusted me.

I completed a TEFL certificate and joined a programme that would place me in a school in China, alongside other teachers from across the world. The very first night when I got to Beijing, I met my roommates, and we went out for dinner. One of my roommates, who was from Blackpool, UK, and around my age, was trying to order plain rice and chicken and the waiters couldn't understand her. Luckily, one of my other roommates from Australia knew a little bit of Mandarin so was able to help.

There were lots of pointing at pictures and sign language, but we got there in the end — so we thought! The waiter came out with a whole chicken head and big feet on a plate. My shocked roommate said, "I'm not eating that." Hiding my desire to laugh out loud, I said, "Yes you are," and I put a piece of lettuce over the chicken's head. It was hilarious.

After a few days in Beijing, I had to make a big choice. We all had to select the age range of students we wanted to teach and what part of China we would prefer to be placed in. There was lots of excitement in the air when our placements were announced on big boards in the hotel lobby. I didn't get the age group I wanted to teach; I got placed in a kindergarten school where the kids were aged one to eight.

With the TEFL training, I thought I was prepared for all age groups. We were taught to sing songs to help learning for this age group and because this was my first experience of teaching, I did that. I did my best as a teacher, but they weren't very happy with me because I didn't teach the way they wanted me to teach. They held meetings about what to do with me because they didn't want to sack me. This was hard to deal with as a 19-year-old as I wanted to prove myself and I wasn't doing well.

They hired a second teacher to help me, but she didn't speak any English and that created a communication problem. I was told that she was an award-winning English teacher, but it was still difficult to understand her. It was a challenge at the beginning but her English improved and so did my teaching over time. This was partly because of her support and partly because the kindergarten gave me some guidelines and books and told me what to teach the kids. I also believe that my determination to be the best teacher I could be helped.

It was distressing at times because while being worried about my performance as a teacher, I got sick often. After all, there was a hole in the wall of our flat where the cold air got in. It was minus 20 degrees in the winter and the kindergarten gave you a limited number of days off before they sacked you.

Some things I handled because I was there, and I had to sort the problems out. I was determined to not only survive there but to make the experience the best I could. Having Ben there also helped massively.

I met Ben, another teacher on the programme, in Beijing. We spoke a couple of times and had an eye on each other. He got placed at a school somewhere completely different to mine, which was at the other end of the country. At 4am on the day, as we were all due to depart for our schools, Ben and I were both put on the bus to Shenyang.

When we got to Shenyang, Ben had to persuade me a little bit to go on a date with him. I thought he was a little bit of a player. I eventually agreed to a date when we were in Shenyang. As soon as we started talking properly, I realised he wasn't a player; he was being sincere.

One challenge we faced was my roommate, who had split up with her boyfriend and then got jealous of my relationship with Ben. From my perspective, we tried our hardest as a new couple to make her feel included. We wouldn't sit on the same sofa when she was in the room, we bought presents for her when we were out, and we always cooked for her, except when we celebrated our one-month anniversary and she got annoyed at that.

It was character-building. The teaching experience helped me grow into myself a bit more. I'm tall and blonde, and not many people in China are, and I stood out everywhere I went. The experience helped me get more comfortable, not just with my looks, but with my perspective on being a Westerner. It helped me be more comfortable with being different. That was something that gave me a lot of confidence. Feeling comfortable in my skin and working as a teacher helped me be comfortable taking the lead to speak in front of people and be a bit more assertive.

I believed in myself, and it was quite hard in many ways. The experience showed me that I can do this, I can make decisions, and I will back myself and get through what I need to get through. I came away with a quiet inner confidence that I can handle it. I can take care of myself. I can overcome obstacles if I need to, I can talk to lots of different nationalities and take on new perspectives since it enhances openness to new ways of life.

The biggest decision I made through my travels was to connect my life and my future to things that just completely altered the path I would have taken, the places I would have left and would have seen. I think that was a big mission.

One of those decisions was giving a relationship with Ben a chance. After we finished our teaching programme, Ben went on to the rest of his gap year and I went back to Sweden. I worked for a short time and then met up with Ben again in Australia. That's where we celebrated our six months anniversary, driving along the Gold Coast in a tiny car. We stayed in Australia for four months, travelling, looking for work and having a good time meeting his relatives. It was the first time I met his dad.

We went on a road trip for a few weeks along the Gold Coast before Ben went back to England. I went back to Sweden briefly and then flew to England to meet his family. In the Autumn of 2011, we both started university in Bangor, Wales. We were there for three years and got our undergraduate degrees, and then we moved to Stockholm. We've been together since and got married in 2017. We recently celebrated three years of marriage, 11 years as a couple, and have a little boy that's one.

The whole trip has been one defining moment. It has shaped who I am, in so many small ways. I now have a job where I work with and help lots of people and need to be able to talk and work with everyone. My solo trip to China prepared me well to do that.

My three tips for an aspiring solo female traveller:

1. Just go for it. Don't overthink it.
2. Make sure you have it roughly planned out. But be flexible and open to new opportunities at the same time.
3. Under-pack rather than over-pack. You can always buy stuff at your destination.

Emma Åsberg Cronshaw is a physiotherapist from Sweden, currently living in Stockholm, although she has lived and worked in many countries from Asia and Australia to Europe. Soon to be a mum of two, she is 31 years old and enjoys spending time outdoors, running, and taking kickboxing classes in her free time.

BEING AWAKE, ALIVE, AND PRESENT

Phillippa Lennon

It was 2004, and I was studying for a master's in counselling psychology. Alongside my studies, I was counselling clients facing significant life challenges, including bereavement and divorce. At a certain point, I realised that I was going to be a qualified psychologist by age 24, technically ready to facilitate change in others, but inside, I felt I needed more life experience to discover what truly creates healing, empowerment, and transformation.

I felt an inner knowing that I would go to India. I wanted to go somewhere I could be of service and make a positive difference in people's lives. I was inspired by Mother Teresa, and growing up, I had heard stories of her charity work in Kolkata. I did some research and found an organisation which helped women and children who were victims of abuse and oppression. I resonated with their mission to empower individuals with hope and dignity, and equip them with the confidence, training, and life skills needed to gain independence and lead meaningful lives.

I now had to raise the finances needed to make the trip happen. I spent a couple of months fundraising before I left. I jumped on my bicycle and cycled for hours every day, seeking support from the local community. I shared from my heart about the cause I wanted to support, and I was very touched by people's genuine interest in what I was standing for and their generous support. I contacted local newspapers, and they were very happy to share my story. This helped raise awareness of what I was doing, inspiring more interest and support. By the time I was ready to fly to

India, I felt physically and mentally very fit, strong, and full of hope and optimism.

I flew to India without any expectations but with the conviction that this was where I was meant to be. When I got off the plane, although I was in a country which was a long way from home with a completely different climate and culture, I immediately felt a sense of familiarity. It was as if on a soul level, I recognised the place. The heat, the sights, the sounds, and the smells that greeted me felt completely different to what I'd known before, and yet, I felt at home in this foreign land and the connection was instant. The energy around me felt chaotic, wild, and intense, yet my body was at ease and my heart was smiling.

Living in India was an adjustment. I lived in a deprived area where there were many people around me living in slums. I didn't have running water and had to go out and gather buckets of cold water to wash myself and my clothes. The noise was incessant. At night, dogs would bark loudly outside my window all night. I dressed in traditional Indian clothes to show respect for the people around me but still, people would stare at me, curious to see a young white woman living in their community.

As soon as I arrived in India, I felt like it pulled me into being fully immersed in the present moment. It awakened all my senses, and the experience was so rich and full that it left me no room for or desire to think about the past or the future. It was as if, in an instant, I left my old life behind and was no longer attached to anything that had come before. Instead, I found myself feeling fully awake, alive, and present. Being there was challenging but it was also intoxicating and exhilarating.

I worked in the women's empowerment organisation for three months and it was a very humbling experience. Working alongside the women was interesting because although we didn't speak the same language, we could still connect through body language, and through being on a journey together. I experienced the power of sisterhood as well as integrating spirituality into my daily life. We did meditation together every morning, and getting into a spiritual morning practice was such a beautiful experience to participate in. If somebody was having a tough day, all the women would come rushing in and support that person.

After working in the women's organisation for the three months, I travelled around India for two weeks. During these two weeks, I travelled through North India and visited places like Darjeeling, Varanasi, Jaipur, and Rishikesh. Throughout my life, I've always been very hardworking and focused on achieving my goals. This was the first time I allowed myself to just let go, trust my instincts, and let life guide me. I was blown away by how colourful India was and how rich and diverse the culture was. Every place I went to offered me a new and enlivening experience. I listened to my intuition and the right people and opportunities always seemed to show up. This was when I got into the flow and adventure of life.

I remember arriving in Jaipur by train late one night. It was late enough that I ought to have been worried because I didn't have anywhere to stay, I didn't have a specific plan, and I was travelling on my own. I got off the train, the station was full of people, and I had different rickshaw drivers bombarding me with requests to go with them. I thought to myself, *What's going to be my next move?* An Australian couple noticed I was on my own and invited me to go with them. I checked in with myself, felt that I didn't want to, and trusted myself to find my own way.

Then, a rickshaw driver called Khan offered to take me to a place to stay. I thought that this was a risky thing to do. However, I checked in with my body and realised that I liked his energy and felt I could trust him. I felt safe to go with him, so I said yes. He helped me to find suitable accommodation, and the next day, he showed me around, taking me to see so many hidden gems that I would never have found on my own. We had so much fun together and he introduced me to so many authentic Indian experiences that I'd never have had if I had chosen to override my intuition and play safe by travelling with the Australian couple. He even let me drive his rickshaw which was a funny and unique experience! Khan and I have remained friends since we met all those years ago! This experience taught me that my intuition is reliable and trustworthy, and I can feel when someone's energy is safe to be with. When I trusted that, I had all sorts of adventures that I wouldn't have experienced if I hadn't said yes to myself and yes to the truth that I felt in my body.

After this experience in India, I returned home to Ireland for Christmas to see family and friends. However, my heart was still in India, and I knew I had tasted something that I wanted more of and needed to explore deeper. After two weeks at home, I decided to travel back to India for another three months; this time, rather than work, I'd allow myself to go on a journey of inward exploration to get to know myself on a deeper level.

I lived in an ashram for three months and engaged in daily meditation, yoga, and spiritual teachings. Outside of the ashram, I did a diploma in ayurvedic massage and studied Reiki levels 1 and 2. These practices have now become part of my life. Choosing to study those Eastern traditional healing practices has impacted my life because I continue to integrate these into my work in the present. I offer different healing practices to my clients and it's also something that informs how I live my life and keep myself in balance and flow.

At the ashram, I made good friends for life. My yoga teacher from the ashram, Amit, and I became good friends and we have met each other in different cities around the world over the years to reconnect, including in New York and London. He encouraged me to dream big, reflected what he viewed as my talents back to me, and talked to me about the impact I could make. Later, when I was living in London, he connected me with different people and gave me opportunities to teach yoga to children and write for a magazine.

Another person who made a big impression on me was a guy called Steve from Australia who was such a free spirit. I loved how adventurous, open-hearted, and present he was. During our time together, he planted seeds in my mind which would later blossom. One of those was how he talked about his experience of living in London, and he suggested that London would be somewhere I'd vibe with from what he knew of me. I trusted him, and at the end of my time in India, I booked a flight to London and made the decision to move there directly from India.

Although Steve returned home to live in Australia, when I arrived in London, I never felt alone because I'd receive regular phone calls from friends of Steve, inviting me out to spend time with them. I was turning up on blind friendship dates, making my initial months in London such a fun and exciting adventure! I'll always be grateful to Steve for the connections I made through his kindness and generosity. That decision to trust Steve and to just relocate to London opened up a whole new world for me. I realised that I could trust life, I'll always meet new people and new opportunities and doors will open up. My move to London became a turning point in my life and London is the place I have chosen to call home since 2006!

As a female solo traveller in India, I needed to be mindful and alert. There were times when I needed to think and act quickly to protect myself. I travelled a lot on trains and buses, often for long journeys lasting several hours, and unfortunately, sometimes I had issues with men attempting to invade my space and cross my physical boundaries. This meant that I had to be in my power, to use my voice, and at times, I had to physically claim my space and push people away. Although this was uncomfortable, I wasn't afraid because, in India, I discovered that I can be very assertive, courageous, and strong. When I need to protect myself, I can take action to do so. As much as India taught me that I can be in the flow, trusting, and intuitive, it also taught me that I can be in my fire, use my voice, and be powerful. This was empowering and made me realise that "I am strong, and I have my own back."

Overall, my time in India felt like embracing the adventure of life. I made so many discoveries and new connections. I remember thinking and feeling, "Wow, how colourful and rich life is; life is such an adventure." I learnt to follow my curiosity and be open to new exciting and inspiring possibilities that come from saying yes to life! I gained spiritual practices that gave me perspective and allowed me to connect with myself as part of the greater whole. These tools enriched my life and the lives of others, as later, I was able to offer them in my work with other people.

My time in India taught me that I only need to play my part by showing up and life will rise to meet me and will give me everything I need. I realised that I don't need to try to control everything, instead, I can be trusting, open, surrender, and allow myself to receive. I learnt that when I trust myself and am open to life, life brings me what is aligned and true for me, and often, what happens is better than I could have imagined. I learnt that I could trust myself, trust my body, my intuition, my decisions, my actions, and life itself. India taught me to live in the present moment, to open my mind and heart, and surrender.

It was my intuition that drew me to India. Everything that flowed from my decision to go to India gave me the feeling that I was exactly where I was meant to be at the right time. India opened my eyes to my courage, power, strength, and the gift of trusting my intuition to guide me. It awakened my senses, honed my intuition, and gave me access to my freedom to choose and co-create my reality in collaboration with life itself. I got an embodied sense of how it is to dance with life freely and to trust it to bring me everything I need. It ignited my fire and passion for being a contribution to others and empowering others to free themselves from fear and limitations, find their voice, passion, and power, and live their truth.

My trip to India was a powerful catalyst for change in my life. It was a steppingstone towards claiming my gifts and my mission to empower others to build healthy, loving, vibrant relationships with themselves, and to feel confident, empowered, and free to choose, as well as create the lives they want. It gave me a lived experience, which showed me that transformation can be deep, profound, graceful, empowering, and fun. This is the experience that I want to offer to my clients as I guide them towards claiming their freedom, power, and purpose. I want to inspire them to connect with the magic and flow of life.

My three tips for an aspiring solo female traveller:

1. Set your intention. Be clear on what your intention is, and what it is that you want to create or experience. Hold that intention in your mind and heart, then surrender to what unfolds.

2. Trust your intuition and your gut feeling; say yes to what feels true in your body. Allow yourself to say yes to yourself and to what feels aligned for you.

3. When you need to speak up for yourself, be courageous and assert yourself. Know that you have the strength inside you to protect yourself and your space. You get to use your voice, be in your power and honour your boundaries.

Phillippa is a Transformational Coach, Relationships Specialist and Holistic Wellbeing Practitioner. Her mission is to empower people to build thriving relationships and lives they are passionate about. She is inspired by nature, travel adventures, books, music and connecting with people.

Website: www.phillippalennon.com
Instagram: @phillippalennon
Facebook: phillippalennon

ANYTHING IS POSSIBLE

Jennifer Schlueter

I was 16 and inspired by the 'anything is possible' culture of the US. I wanted to go on an exchange from Germany to the US. I found a company that placed me with a host family in Orange County for four weeks. The family were kind and loving and so different to my family because my parents are separated. I got to feel what a family is like and what people look like when they're in something together. I found it funny that the mom is Greek, the dad is Danish, and they went to a German bar, both wanting to meet a German but instead found each other!

I was really shy and would barely say anything. They forced me to speak English for those four weeks, and I returned to Germany with a thick American accent and a lot more open and talkative. I began to ask myself if I could make it happen to study and live there.

The difference in lifestyles was crazy. I went to malls, Las Vegas, San Diego, and LA. When my exchange student came over to Germany, it was different for her. She could only do nature walks and explore some cities, which are not comparable. It was sometimes boring for her and there were not many malls around.

When I was 19, I told my mom that I want to go to LA and that I don't want to be in Germany anymore. I was never really close to my family, so it was an easy move for me to make. I packed up my things and I started a completely new life in LA.

When I arrived in LA, I didn't have an apartment booked. The host family from my previous trip thought I was crazy. The mom asked me, "How can you expect that it's just going to fall into your lap?" I held positive thoughts and beliefs that things would fall into place, and it did. My host mom drove me to an international student orientation in LA and where she approached a girl with blonde hair because she thought she was German, which she was, and introduced us. That led to her offering me a room with her for two weeks before I found my apartment.

Thinking positively has accompanied me on all my travels; I believe that everything's always working out for me, and it always does.

The change of location where everything was new made me into the person that I am now; I am confident and clear on who I am and what I want. I would never have had that growth in Germany. The mindset that anything is possible, that whatever you want to do is achievable and even if you think about an idea that sounds crazy to everyone, you can achieve it, was so inspiring.

My confidence came from being thrown into a situation and learning to create a new life. I was in a house with six roommates, and at first, I wouldn't utter a word or a sentence to them because I thought my English was bad, and I was shy. I thought I had nothing to say. They would invite me out and I would go and talk to new people to make friends. I had to get around and find what I needed by myself in a completely different country which developed my confidence.

Then I became more body confident. Growing up in Germany as a teenager was tough. There was this image of what a beautiful woman was, someone who had big boobs, blonde hair, and no arse. I was not that at all. In LA, I felt people appreciated my body, and it didn't matter what I looked like, I was still beautiful.

It didn't matter that I didn't fit into these German beauty standards, some people found me attractive in LA. I noticed that LA had a spectrum of people from the worst people you can ever meet, as in murderers and gang members, to the best people you could ever meet as in very inspiring entrepreneurs, very incredibly driven, ambitious people who just made it happen from zero. I know immigrants, from Iran, Lebanon, and other places who made a good life for themselves there.

My former boss was an immigrant from Iran and had made it for himself. We were sitting in a café one day and I said, "Oh my god, I'm so worried because I don't know if I'm going to get a work visa or not and I want to stay, I want to set it up," and what he said stuck with me. He said, "Why are you thinking about the negatives and the negative outcomes, why are you not thinking that you're going to get it? Why are you not thinking that you can do anything and that anything is possible?" That moment has stuck with me to this day. Whenever I ask myself if I can do something, I remember his words and I think, *Of course, I can. Why not?!*

Towards the last two years of my life in LA, I was the managing editor of 22 newspapers, and it was a great job. It taught me a lot, but I was only 25 at the time. I had a car in LA, an apartment, friends, and an amazing life, but at the same time, something was missing. Freedom was missing. I was only able to go on five days of paid vacation in a year. I'm a traveller at heart and grew up in Europe where I travelled a lot. I decided I wanted more holidays, and I didn't want to be limited to the income I was getting.

My friend suggested seeing a hypnotherapist, and even though I didn't know what it entailed, I went. The morning after the first hypnosis session, I woke up and decided to quit my job and go to Paris for six months. I called my friend and told her about my decision, and she said, "Jenny, why are you limiting yourself, why not the world?" which is a typical US response. I decided to quit my job and travel the world after my first and last hypnotherapy session. Six months later, I was on the road, and I've been travelling ever since.

I don't have much fear. I have a strong will. I had the will to leave Germany, I had the will to explore the world, and I had the will to do something that nobody else would do. My will was stronger than my fear. It wasn't the mindset that everything was going to work out, it was just the will; I was determined to make it happen for me.

Vaishali Patel

My three tips for an aspiring solo female traveller:

1. Really listen to your intuition. If your gut tells you something is off, something is off. If your gut tells you something about a person is not right, it isn't, so really listen to your intuition.
2. Don't plan, because as soon as you are in a city, you will meet people and they will invite you to things, which will just really make your day, and everything that you want to do will somehow fall into place. Just put it out in the universe and whatever you want will fall into place.
3. Make friends with locals, don't stick to your ex-pat crowd, and don't stick to the people you know. Meet the locals, hang out and do things with them. Get to know them, get to know the traditions and festivals and all of that. You might get invited into a family home for food, where you'll get to know so much more.

After her first hypnosis session, Jennifer Schlueter quit her job as Managing Editor of 22 newspapers to travel the world while working online. She became a certified hypnotherapist herself and teaches Spiritual Hypnosis while traveling with a base in South Africa.

*Instagram: @jenniferschlueter_*

CONCLUSION

Dear reader,

I hope you have enjoyed reading the inspiring, hand-picked stories that I have brought together in this travel anthology. It has been a labour of love, and my primary intention was to empower women [and men] like you to embrace solo travel as a transformative journey of self-discovery.

Through these pages, I wanted to remind you of the incredible potential that solo travel holds. It's not just about exploring new places; it's about embarking on an inner adventure that can change your life in profound ways. As you read the stories of these brave women, I trust you found ones that resonated with you, providing courage, inspiration, and a sense of camaraderie.

I know that, sometimes, the idea of solo travel can be daunting. Safety concerns, self-doubt, and fears of the unknown may hold you back. But take heart from these women's experiences — some of them, too, faced similar worries, and yet they leapt into the unknown, transforming their lives through the journey.

Each story in this book is a testament to the power of travel to broaden horizons, challenge preconceptions, and instil life-changing skills like self-trust, resilience, and adaptability. I wanted to create a space where you could find wisdom, practical tips, and encouragement to embark on your own solo adventure, irrespective of where you are in life or your level of travel experience.

Remember, this journey of exploration is unique to you. If you are an experienced solo traveller, may these stories serve as a reminder of your own strength and resilience.

I hope you now feel ready to embark on your own journey. You now hold within you a treasure trove of inspiration, guidance, and encouragement. Trust yourself, have a loose plan in place, make connections, and embrace the adventure with confidence.

Let this book be your companion as you step into the world with curiosity and openness, ready to discover the enchantment that awaits you.

Thank you for joining me and these incredible women on this transformative journey. May it inspire you to explore the world, connect with diverse cultures, and, most importantly, find a deeper connection with yourself.

I invite you to share your own transformative solo travel stories with me. Your experiences may inspire others and even find their place in the next edition of this book. I look forward to hearing how this book had an impact on you.

Also, if you'd like to talk to me about how you can plan a transformative and meaningful solo travel experience or you would like to invite me to speak about the power of solo travel, then don't hesitate to get in touch with me at:

vaishali@solo-explorers.com
Instagram: solo.explorers

Explore a variety of free resources at www.solo-explorers.com to enhance your solo travel experience.

Bon voyage!
With warmth and empowerment,
Vaishali Patel

ACKNOWLEDGEMENTS

With heartfelt gratitude, I wish to express my deepest thanks to the many individuals who played an instrumental role in bringing this book to fruition.

First and foremost, I extend my appreciation to Mark Julian Edwards for his unwavering support and encouragement, which served as a source of inspiration, reminding me that I could indeed accomplish this feat. Mark, your introductions to some of the remarkable women featured in the book have been invaluable.

I would also like to extend my gratitude to Pat Finn of Rubicon Results, whose coaching and accountability were instrumental in completing this project. Pat, your connections and introductions to several of the individuals featured in the book have greatly enriched its content.

A heartfelt thank you goes to Marie Soprovich of the GIFEW network for introducing me to some of the inspiring individuals featured in the book.

To the incredible women whose stories grace these pages, your courage, wisdom, and resilience serve as beacons of inspiration. I am deeply humbled by the privilege of sharing your transformative journeys, and I'm grateful for your invaluable input in shaping the book.

My sincere appreciation extends to my family and friends for their continuous support and encouragement. Special thanks to Minalkumar Patel, whose diligent proofreading during a flight to New York was a tremendous help.

I must acknowledge the entire publishing team at Balboa for their dedication and expertise to bring this book to life. I'm particularly grateful to Tamarind Hill Press Limited (THPeditingServc) for their exceptional editorial and proofreading services.

My heartfelt thanks also go to Alessandra Alonso, Meera Dattani, Jake Haupert, and Noo Saro-Wiwa for their gracious endorsements.

Victoria von Stein, your valuable insights and contributions to the front cover design are deeply appreciated.

And to my Facebook community, thank you for your invaluable input in helping me choose a book title. Your support has been a crucial part of this journey.

ABOUT THE AUTHOR

Vaishali is an avid solo traveler and transformation expert with a keen interest in how travel, creativity, and well-being can open new realms of potential. Vaishali believes that venturing beyond our comfort zones through solo travel provides us with insights into both us and the world around us. These insights play a pivotal role in shaping our aspirations and influencing our perspectives.

Reflecting on her own experiences, Vaishali shares, "My solo expeditions throughout my 20s and 30s not only catalyzed my career in marketing but also bolstered my self-confidence. I am enthusiastic about extending these benefits to others, allowing them to thrive in similar ways."

She shares her own journey through a TEDx talk called 'Your Body's Intelligence' and now coaches people to embrace their genuine self-expression, be that public speaking or travelling solo.

Explore a variety of free resources at www.solo-explorers.com to enhance your solo travel experience.

Printed in Great Britain
by Amazon

36439717R00097